To Marga[illegible]
with H[illegible]

12/25/98

INSPIR[illegible], ACTS OF HEALING, PROPHECY, AND TRANSFORMATION FOR OUR CONTEMPORARY TIMES

Here are over fifty true encounters of ordinary men and women touched by the extraordinary in their everyday lives. Read about . . .

- **The woman who, acting on the Lord's directions, rescues an elderly couple from a raging inferno.**
- **How one woman's faith in God heals her body on the eve of surgery.**
- **The prophetic messages from a portrait of Jesus that help a metaphysical healer bring her patients astounding results.**
- **The altered state of consciousness that allows a young woman to exorcise a dark spirit from the soul of an elderly friend.**

And . . .

- **The softspoken hitchhiker with long hair and penetrating eyes who appears bathed in a blue-white light, and saves people's lives—only to vanish without a trace.**

He Walks with Me

True Encounters with Jesus

Brad Steiger and
Sherry Hansen Steiger

A SIGNET BOOK

SIGNET
Published by the Penguin Group
Penguin Putnam Inc., 375 Hudson Street,
New York, New York 10014, U.S.A.
Penguin Books Ltd, 27 Wrights Lane,
London W8 5TZ, England
Penguin Books Australia Ltd, Ringwood,
Victoria, Australia
Penguin Books Canada Ltd, 10 Alcorn Avenue,
Toronto, Ontario, Canada M4V 3B2
Penguin Books (N.Z.) Ltd, 182–190 Wairau Road,
Auckland 10, New Zealand

Penguin Books Ltd, Registered Offices:
Harmondsworth, Middlesex, England

First published by Signet, an imprint of Dutton Signet,
a member of Penguin Putnam Inc.

First Printing, May, 1998
10 9 8 7 6 5 4 3 2 1

Printed in the United States of America

Contents

CHAPTER ONE

"Lo, I Am with You Always"

Before he ascended into heaven after his crucifixion and resurrection, Jesus promised his disciples—and in turn, all those who would call upon his name—that he would be with them until the end of the world. Throughout history, Christians have taken their savior at his word and have expressed their faith by calling upon Jesus to hear and to answer their prayers.

Down through the ages, a number of devout practitioners of the Christian faith have claimed to have seen Jesus during ecstatic encounters or crisis experiences. In recent years, however, manifestations of the physical person and/or the holy image of Jesus have been steadily increasing.

Many sincere Christians are convinced that such

sightings herald the End Times, the advent of the Millennium when Jesus promised to return in the clouds with his angelic host to set in motion the apocalyptic march to Armageddon and Judgment Day.

Others feel that the Master Jesus is appearing now to signal a time of transition for all of humankind as our entire species approaches the advent of the next step forward in our spiritual evolution.

Since the early 1970s, we have received numerous accounts from people who claim direct contact and personal interaction with Jesus. These "Close Encounters of the Divine Kind" have occurred to churched and unchurched alike and to individuals of all ages, ethnic backgrounds, and socioeconomic status.

According to the thousands of respondents of our questionnaire of mystical and paranormal occurrences—as well as those men and women who have personally told us their stories—Jesus has appeared to bring spiritual wisdom and counsel, messages of inspiration, acts of healing, prophetic warnings, and personal transformation.

Jesus Appears in Church to Heal Her Injured Leg

A woman we shall call Jeanette was kneeling alone at prayer in a Catholic church. When she looked up, she saw Jesus in fleshly form, his head bowed, staring at her. As she watched, he lifted his head slowly and closed his eyes.

For the first time, she noticed that his outstretched arms indicated the position in which they would have been pinioned to the cross. With a slight gasp, he turned his head to the right side, and Jeanette felt as if she was watching her Savior die on the cross.

Seconds later the vision had disappeared, but Jeanette now became aware that the severe pain in her left leg—the one that had been broken and needed surgery in order to be correctly reset—was no longer troubling her. In fact, she was able to walk the six blocks to her apartment without the slightest discomfort.

Three days later, her puzzled physician agreed that the damaged leg had somehow corrected itself. Her vision of Jesus had manifested a miracle healing.

Embraced by the Light of the Lord

Mark, a security guard in Los Angeles, said that late one night as he was checking the darkened warehouse assigned to his care, he encountered the glowing figure of Jesus.

"I had really been depressed," he said. "I felt that my life had taken so many turns for the worse that there really was no point in going on with my miserable existence.

"Then, suddenly, right before me—where there had been nothing but darkness—I saw Jesus. His clothing was a robe of a soft white color. His hair was long, down to his shoulders, and both his hair and his beard were a golden brown in color. He was surrounded by a brilliant light that circled him like a big halo. Behind him was a kind of rainbow of colors.

"He opened his arms wide, as if to embrace me, and I wanted to go to him and let him put his arms around me. I hesitated, though, feeling uncertain of just what I should do, what would be proper. Mentally, I heard him say that he loved me and that everything would soon be all right. In the next second, he was gone, and I just stood there crying for about half an hour.

"I really felt like a new person after Jesus left. I felt as though I had been reborn. Things did get better for me in the next few days, and I will always know in my heart and soul that I really saw Jesus in that warehouse that night. I will never forget his appearance and his words that he loved me."

A "Burning Coal" Gave Him the Tongue of an Angel

An Episcopalian priest told us that he was awakened one night by the image of Jesus, who placed a kind of "burning coal" on his lips.

"I began to speak. My wife woke up and she heard me speaking in what she later said was the strangest, most beautiful language that she had ever heard."

The next day, during his meeting with the bishop, he eloquently expressed his congregation's needs and won his superior's support for greater financial aid.

"I know that without the appearance of Jesus and his help, I would have been intimidated, tongue tied, and argued ineffectually with the bishop for my cause," the priest said.

An "Electric Shock" from Jesus Removed His Addictions

A young salesman told us how he had been mired in the despair of drug addiction and alcoholism. He asked if we would believe that he, who now stood before us in glowing health and vigor, had been reduced to a shaking skeleton that barely weighed a hundred pounds. What had happened to him? What transforming influence and power had redeemed him from a miserable and ignoble death?

He had walked into a dirty, dingy motel room with a bottle and his usual bad attitude. Someone had left a Gideon Bible open on the bed. As he bent down to move it aside, certain words in the text seemed to be glowing a bright red.

"They were the words of Jesus when he said, 'Lo, I am with you always, even to the end of the world.'

"I mumbled something about how Jesus certainly had never been with me—and then there was a brilliant flash of light and He stood there before me! I fell to my knees and wept aloud: 'Help me, Jesus! I am a wretched excuse for one of God's children!'

"He reached out to touch me, and it was like electricity going through me. I felt pure, God-energy moving through every cell of my body.

"Jesus was gone in the next blink of an eye—but he took all my addictions, all my pain, and all my weaknesses with him. I have not taken any drugs or alcohol since that day eleven years ago."

Jesus Cured Klara's Addictions "Cold Turkey"

A young addict named Klara told us how she had been on drugs for two years, then went "cold turkey" one night in a Detroit jail after calling on Jesus.

In a moving, personal account, she said, "And He came, and He changed me right then and there."

She Called on Jesus to Deliver Her from Evil

Sally and her husband moved into an old farmhouse in Montana when she was a twenty-three-year-old mother with a two-year-old son and another child on the way.

"The third night we slept in that old house, I was awakened in the middle of the night by an awful feeling of fear," she said. "I sat up in bed, turned on the light, and was terrified by what I saw. A dark, shadowy shape was moving toward us through the closed bedroom door. I sensed violent anger and terrible evil coming from it, and I was paralyzed with fear. I felt as though I was being held down and smothered."

Sally said that it took all of her strength to call upon the name of Jesus to protect her from evil. "At that very next moment, a bright light appeared just above the hideous dark entity. I knew that it was Jesus manifesting in answer to my prayer—and so did the evil creature. It fled from the room and seemed to disappear."

Sally got out of bed and grabbed her sleeping son from his baby bed. "The light of Christ stayed for just a little while longer, then it, too, vanished. I woke up my husband, told him what had happened, and we both prayed until nearly dawn. We were never bothered again by that awful thing as long as we lived in that old farmhouse. It was Jesus who taught us to pray to be delivered from evil, and I am grateful that I remembered to pray his prayer that horrible night."

Jesus Appeared to Pope Pius XII

At the height of his illness in December 1954, Pope Pius XII had a vision of Jesus in which the Savior spoke to him in "His own true voice." The Vatican kept Pius's revelation secret for nearly a year, then through the "affectionate indiscretion" of one of the Holy Father's close friends, the magazine *Oggi* broke the story in its November 19, 1955 issue.

On December 12, the Vatican confirmed the remarkable disclosure, declaring the vision not to have been a dream. Sources near to the pope said that he had been wide awake and lucid.

Vatican authorities said that there had not been a more vivid or specific vision of Jesus since the days of the Apostles than that reported by the pontiff. According to their records, Christ had appeared to a pope only once before, and that was in the fourth century, when Pope Sylvester consecrated the mother church of St. John Lateran in Rome after Emperor Constantine had ended the brutal persecutions of the Christians.

Roman Catholic scholarship holds that there are two kinds of visions:

One is the imaginative vision, in which the object seen is but a mental concept or symbol, such as Jacob's Ladder leading up to Heaven. St. Teresa of Avila had numerous visions, including images of Christ, which Church authorities have judged were of this symbolic kind of vision.

The other is the corporeal vision, in which the figure seen is externally present or in which a supernatural power has so modified the retina of the eye so as to produce the effect of three-dimensional solidarity.

In the twelfth century, St. Francis of Assisi was credited with seeing Christ. St. Catherine of Sienna reported seeing Christ in the fourteenth century. The Catholic devotion to the Sacred Heart as a symbol of love was begun in the seventeenth century after the vision of Christ had been seen by the French nun St. Margaret Mary.

A Great Evangelical Protestant Meets Jesus "Face to Face"

Charles G. Finney is considered by some to be among the greatest evangelists since the days of the Apostles. Scholar James Gilchrist Lawson considers Finney's *Systematic Theology* to be "probably the greatest work on theology outside of the Scriptures."

But Finney was once a skeptical law student. It was one morning in the autumn of 1821, while on his way to study law in the office of Squire Wright in western New York, that he had a vision of Jesus hanging on the cross. That night after dinner, he stepped out of his office into a dark room and "met the Lord Jesus Christ face to face."

Finney later wrote that he saw him as he would any other man. Jesus did not speak, but looked at Finney in such a manner that the young lawyer fell down at his feet and wept. A few moments later, he received a "mighty baptism of the Holy Ghost," which descended on him in a manner that seemed to go through him "body and soul." Finney said that he could feel the energy, "like a wave of electricity going through and through" him, like waves of "liquid love," like "the very breath of God."

Why shouldn't such visions of Jesus continue to manifest?

A Life-Altering Experience for a Chicago CEO

A corporate executive in Chicago told us of a life-altering experience that occurred when he was twenty-seven and received a vision of Jesus reaching out to him. "I seemed to 'feel' rather than hear His message. He told me that he was more than a good teacher who had done good works. He was the Son of the Living God, who had died for my sins.

"That message brought me into a vital, personal relationship with Jesus. I absolutely *knew* that Jesus loved me, that he had given himself for me, that he would come to my life personally and really change my life if I would allow him to do so. I did accept Jesus as my savior, and my life changed completely from that moment on."

An Attorney in Washington, D.C. Receives Messages from Jesus

James E. Padgett, an attorney in Washington, D.C., received messages from Jesus that gave him spiritual courage and guided both his life and the lives of many others through difficult times.

In the following brief excerpt, Jesus speaks of *The Power of Love to Redeem Men and Women from Sin and Error:*

> My Father's love is . . . the only thing in all the universe that can save humans from their evil natures and make them at one with Him. This Divine Love is the one great power that moves the universe, and without it there would not be the wonderful harmony that exists in the Celestial Heavens of the spirit world—nor would so much happiness exist among angels who inhabit these spheres. Only this Divine Love can . . . make people like the Father in Love and happiness and harmony. This Love has no counterpart in all creation, and comes from the Father alone . . . This Love

has the power to change the most hardened sinner into a true child of God.

Fifty Years of Ecstasy and Peaceful Calm

A successful businessman in Illinois told us how his acceptance of Jesus in his teenage years had stood him in good stead all of his life.

"When I was fifteen years old and attending a Baptist church service, the minister gave the call to come down and make a confession of faith. I recall very vividly that I decided that was the right thing to do.

"I'll never forget how a fountain of light seemed to open up inside of me, and I heard beautiful singing and a voice that said to me, 'I am Jesus. If you will always listen to my word, everything will always be all right.'

"In the fifty years or so that have passed, I have learned to listen and to experience the tremendous ecstasy and the calming peace within me. I believe that this peace and calm is something that all people might receive if they prepare themselves through prayer and study and are willing to listen to the words of Jesus within their hearts."

But Are All These People Really Seeing the True Jesus?

In his thoughtful book, *The Meeting of Science and Spirit: Guidelines for a New Age,* author John White argues that when Jesus "went to prepare a place" for his followers by ascending to the Father, he "dissolved utterly out of time and space, leaving not the slightest trace—physical or psychic—behind. He . . . returned to the glory which He had with God 'before the world was.' He vanished entirely out of space—

time, ceasing to exist in any form whatsoever. He returned wholly to the Formless state of being."

What, then, in White's view, do people experience when they see Jesus in visions, meditations, or dreams?

> An image from their own minds. But I am not denigrating that image because the image is not based on fantasy or imagination in the ordinary sense of those words. It *is* from a higher level of reality, but it is not ultimate.

White reminds his readers "how much thought and thought-energy has been directed by people around the world to the life of Jesus—especially to the idea of Jesus as the Perfect Human." It is, therefore, a psychologically created thought form of the romanticized Jesus that people see.

> It is a composite picture built up over the centuries from the mental impressions of millions and millions of people who—through prayer, study, and heartfelt yearning for self-transcendence via the Christian path—have unknowingly added their psychic energy to a worldwide field of thought energy and thereby built up a "charged" repository of "mindstuff" which stores the image holographically in a planetary thoughtfield. That repository is accessible to people in altered states of consciousness.

White feels that the same psychic mechanism exists even for those who claim to see Jesus in their waking state. "It is simply the externalization of their own subconscious but mistaken mind-image." As such, White hastens to add:

> It is not "wrong"—it is simply nonultimate. It is spiritually valid, but only as a phenomenon characteristic of an intermediate stage of unfoldment. It is a form of experience to be understood and transcended.

In White's opinion what is truly unique about Jesus is that he was the first to transcend his physical body, even his light-body, and totally, utterly "return to the Father," the prior and primal condition of all the universe.

> No matter how that return is viewed, Jesus "saved" the world by showing the Way and making it possible for the entire human race to be Christed. His "return to glory" paradoxically places him here in the world more truly, more fully than if he were still residing in a body of light-energy and located somewhere in space . . . As Jesus of Nazareth, he is to be found nowhere. As a manifestation of the Christic state, he is to be found everywhere and has been since the beginning of time . . .
>
> Thus the historical Jesus does not exist as a spirit entity. Jesus will not return to Earth on a cloud with angels playing trumpets because he is here already—in the very center of you and me as our deepest nature, our very essence. Instead of being *somewhere,* he is *everywhere* . . . He is in our mind and hearts, our blood and DNA and nervous system, our relationships and aspirations and ideals, beckoning at the doorway of higher consciousness

> for us to open it and enter, that we might realize our true self, ascend through evolution to godhead and become "one in Christ."

While John White's thoughts are provocative, we know from our many years of friendship that he seeks always to encourage his readers to be open minded rather than dogmatic. In Chapter 23 "The Meaning of the Christ" in his book *The Meeting of Science and Spirit,* he concedes that it is "theoretically possible" that the historical Jesus has chosen to remain on Earth as a spiritual entity.

"Even the gospels," he writes, "tell us that Jesus said, 'Lo, I am with you always, even unto the end of the age.' In some sense, Jesus has never left us."

"By Their Fruits You Shall Know Them"

Some years ago, while interviewing Diane Kennedy Pike on the question of revelation and revelators, she stated that while most Christians agree that Jesus is alive in some sense and with them on some level of reality, she felt certain that He would be highly selective in his choice of a revelator so that His message would not be distorted unduly.

"Many times people seem to get into mental things that are really out of their own idea realm," she said. "They think they are communicating with [Jesus], but really they are not. My personal feeling is that the test that Jesus gave is really the safest one, and that is you can really know the difference by the person's life.

> "Beware of false prophets . . . Ye shall know them by their fruits . . . A good tree cannot bring forth

> evil fruit, neither can a corrupt tree bring forth good fruit . . . Wherefore, by their fruits ye shall know them."—Matthew 7:15–20, King James Version

"I think that people who have received a revelation from the Higher Realm will manifest high characteristics or qualities in their life or understanding," she continued. "There will emerge in them a deeper sense of peace as a result of their communication and a deeper sense of wholeness. Physical health will begin to manifest.

"People who are on their own ego trip will manifest what we call ego qualities—deceptiveness, self-assertiveness, pride, and so forth, which are not really characteristics of higher developed spiritual people.

"And I think anything that is fear oriented," she added, "is obviously not of the higher realm. A so-called revelation that indicates that you should fear something coming to you from somewhere else or that incites fear in other people when you tell them about it is not from a Higher Being."

"Lo, I Am with You Always"

In his venerable book of Bible commentary, *Halley's Bible Handbook,* Henry H. Halley declares that the Christian's favorite verse in the entire Bible has to be Matthew 28:20, in which Jesus promises, "I am with you always."

> Jesus rose, nevermore to die. He is *alive* now, and is with his people, in guiding and protecting power, all the time.

> . . . Jesus said it in the plainest possible language, *"I am with you all the time."* He meant something when he said that, and we believe that, in some real sense, beyond our comprehension, mystic, but real, *He* is with each one of us all the time.
>
> No matter how weak or humble or unimportant, *He* is our friend, our companion. Invisible, but there. Now, right now. Tonight, while we are asleep. Tomorrow, while we are at work . . . Shadowing us through life. Walking by our side. Watching with kindly interest every detail of life's pitiful struggle, trying so patiently to lead us up to a place of immortal happiness in His Father's home.

In Brad Steiger's *Revelation: The Divine Fire,* Dr. Richard L. Rubenstein, professor of psychology of religion at Florida State University in Tallahassee, commented on the rise of Pentecostal and charismatic church movements and the growing popularity of experiential phenomena in religion:

> When all of the traditional ways of seeing reality as ultimately guided by a Divine Destiny no longer work, people are not going to be satisfied with living in a world in which God is not present in any sense. The world is capped and in some sense completed by the presence of God or the presence of Jesus. This need to experience God or to experience Jesus becomes very important.
>
> Once you have the "Death of God" theologians who speak of the absence of God and once it becomes difficult intellectually to argue against such people, then the next step is liable to be: 'Well, I

can't argue intellectually . . . but I *have experienced* God in my life!' This, therefore, is a shift from the intellect to experience."

While Professor Rubenstein admits that he has never had such a personal interaction with the presence of Jesus, he states that he would never say to a person who says that in some sense he has experienced God or he has experienced Jesus that he was wrong. "Because the only way to know what such a person is talking about is to have the experience that he has experienced."

"He walks with me, and He talks with me, and He tells me I am His own."

—From the popular hymn, *The Garden*

While each reader must make his or her own assessment of these personal accounts of men and women who sincerely believe that they have walked and talked with Jesus in dreams, visions, or physical materializations, we can promise that the stories shared in this book will provide inspiration, comfort, guidance, and perhaps even illumination.

CHAPTER TWO

✠

Dreams of Jesus and His Abiding Love

Many readers of this book may be familiar with the questionnaire of mystical experiences that we have been distributing since the late 1960s. In the section regarding dreams, we ask such questions as the following:

- *Have you ever had dreams in which you seemed to be watching yourself in what appears to be biblical times, communicating with religious figures from that historical period?*
- *Have you ever had dreams in which you communicated with angelic or holy figures?*
- *Have you ever dreamed of visiting heaven or paradise?*

During the past thirty years, we have given the questionnaire to more than twenty thousand readers of our books and members of our lecture or seminar audiences, and we have received hundreds of truly remarkable accounts of dramatic encounters with the unseen dimensions and realities of our universe. While large portions of the questionnaire are composed of queries that may be answered with a check mark or a simple "yes" or "no," we encourage respondents to take as many extra sheets of paper as necessary to detail some of their more complex or life-altering experiences.

Here are just a few inspirational accounts selected from the files of hundreds of questionnaire respondents who shared their personal stories of profound dreams of Jesus and His abiding, unconditional love:

A Vivid Dream of Meeting Jesus in an Empty Church

When Patrick, a real estate agent from Colorado, was just a boy of five, he received his awakening into a higher awareness because of a very vivid dream of Jesus.

In Patrick's own words, here are the details of that singular dream that influenced a young boy's reality and set the course for his life path in adulthood:

> I dreamed that I was sitting alone in our church when Jesus came out of a narrow door behind me. I sat on the bench, waiting for him. I remained very still as he moved around the bench toward me.
>
> At first I was afraid of him. I mean, he was Jesus in person, after all. He seemed really tall to me. He had long brown, almost black, shoulder-length hair and a beard. It seems to me that he might

have carried a long staff in one hand, but I'm not certain.

When he sat down and looked at me, however, all fear melted away. His eyes were so loving, so kind, so peaceful.

Then he began to talk with me—but not with his mouth, with his mind. I could hear and understand everything at the time. He spoke of so many beautiful things and wonderful truths. He told me that I had a mission to perform on Earth, and he asked me to promise him that I would try always to help others less fortunate than myself.

Now, years later, I can't remember too much of what Jesus said. I know there was a lot more that I remembered at the time, but I have since forgotten with my conscious memory recall. But I will never forget the love that I felt flowing from him into me! My remembrance of his loving eyes has been my mental harbor during many a terrible crisis.

Jesus and an Angel Showed Her Her Name in the Book of Life

"For forty years now, people have been telling me that it must have been a dream; but I will always believe that it was a real experience with Jesus," Joyce, an elementary school teacher from Oklahoma, began her story:

I was four, maybe five, years old. I had just said my bedtime prayers, and I clearly remember wondering if Jesus was really listening and—most of all—if Jesus really cared for me. I had overheard my parents and my Uncle Burt talking after dinner that night, and, to put it diplomatically, Burt was a borderline atheist.

Anyway, I fell asleep, worrying about my place in Jesus' scheme of things. Later, I was awakened by someone calling my name.

Now, I will swear that I was fully awake when I turned over and clearly saw Jesus and an angel standing beside my bed. Mom always clicked on my Yogi Bear—or whoever it was—nightlight, and I could distinctly see these two majestic figures in my little room standing in the soft glow of that light.

Jesus smiled at me, then beckoned for the angel to step closer to my bedside. The angel was dressed in really bright white robes and he or she had a very full set of wings. When the heavenly being drew nearer, I saw that he held a large book in his hands.

Jesus nodded at the angel, and he took a feather pen from behind his ear and pointed with its tip at something he had written in the book. I leaned forward and saw that he had written my name. The angel smiled at me, looked up at Jesus—and they both disappeared.

Even then I understood that Jesus was showing me that I did matter to him and that my name was recorded in His big Book of Life. I have never forgotten this vision of belonging to Jesus, and it has comforted me often during difficult times on my earthly path.

Seeing the Sadness in Jesus' Eyes Inspired Him to Help Others

Robert, a social worker from Kentucky, remembers that he was sixteen when he awakened one night to see Jesus and two angels standing in his bedroom:

> All three of them gave off a tremendously bright white light.
>
> I wasn't afraid, for I knew that Jesus loved me and that his angels watched over me.
>
> I asked Jesus why he had appeared to me. He said nothing, but I saw great sadness in his eyes.
>
> The deeper I looked into his eyes, the more I felt tears begin to run down my cheeks. I had a rush of awareness of all the sorrow that Jesus had seen down through the ages. I had a sense of all the sin and misery that human ignorance had spread throughout the planet with its wars and murders, lies and deceits.
>
> It was at that moment that I heard Jesus speaking to me inside my head. He told me that it was my Earth mission to help the sick and troubled people of the planet. I decided then that I would either become a teacher or a social worker.
>
> As soon as I had formed that thought, the three holy figures vanished. I was left with such a feeling of unconditional love that the sensation almost became unbearable. I didn't fall back asleep for hours.

Was Her Presence at Jesus' Empty Tomb Only a Vivid Dream?

The dream of seeing the empty tomb on the morning of Jesus' resurrection was so vivid that Jennifer, a motel manager from Florida, still wonders if "somehow, in some way, the God force moved me back in time to witness the greatest single event in the history of the world."

Jennifer provided us with a lengthy account of her extraordinary experience:

> I dreamed that I was walking in this lovely garden just as the sun was rising. When I looked around me, I saw that I was walking in the midst of a group of robed women, perhaps as many as twelve. And then I saw that I, too, wore a robe, such as those worn by women in the Middle East.
>
> "Be of good cheer," one of the women said aloud. "Let us dry our tears and remember the Lord's promise to vanquish death."
>
> Another woman shifted the weight of a large ceramic bowl that she carried on her shoulder. "But first death must be dealt with. Our spices shall prepare our Lord's body for his sleep in the tomb, for he is surely dead."
>
> It was as if I had found myself participating in an active scene for which my brain was unprepared. I took note of details a little at a time as I kept pace with the group of women. I now noticed that

they all carried pots and bowls, and I could catch the aroma of strong spices and herbs.

Suddenly I had a flash of realization. The woman who seemed to be the leader of the group was Mary Magdalene. Other names came to me, "Mary," "Salome," "Joanna." I was walking with the women who came to attend to the crucified body of Jesus on Resurrection morning.

My heart pounded my chest as my pulse quickened. This was no dream, I told myself. This was real. The grass beneath my feet. The smell of burial spices. The soft murmurs of solemn conversation. The clear morning sky. The burial caves and tombs scattered around us.

"Look!" one of the women shouted. "The stone has been rolled away."

A number of the women began to weep and moan pitifully. "Where have they taken our Lord's body?"

Mary Magdalene narrowed her large brown eyes in great anger. "Guards were posted to prevent such a thing as this. Can we trust the Roman pigs to do anything right?"

Just then a bright light appeared beside the large rock at the mouth of the tomb. We all shielded our eyes against the brilliance until the light dimmed and we saw that a young man stood before us.

"Why have you come here so early this morning?" he asked us.

"We have come to attend to the body of our Lord," one of the women—I think it was Mary, the mother of James and Joses said.

The handsome young man smiled. "Why do you seek him here in this tomb? This is a place of death. He has risen!"

"Please, young sir," another of the women protested. "Do not jest with us. We are in mourning over the death of our Lord. Please tell us where they have taken him."

Another young man, who was also attired in brilliant white clothing, appeared beside the other. "Please, dear ones, enter the tomb and witness for yourselves and for your brothers who remain in their lodging places. The one you seek, Jesus of Nazareth, is not here. He is risen."

I crowded into the small burial area with the other women. A shroud of coarse linen lay on a slab of rock. There was no body in the tomb.

"It's true!" Mary Magdalene shouted her unrestrained joy. "Our Lord has conquered the death of the tomb, just as he promised. He is risen!"

"Where did those two young men go?" one of the women asked.

"Yes," wondered another. "Who were they? And where could they have gone so quickly? It is as if they disappeared."

"They were angels," I told them, laughing as tears of wonder and joyful affirmation ran down my cheeks. "Those two young men in the bright white robes were angels! We could only see two of them, but there were probably thousands of angels milling around us unseen to celebrate this most glorious of all occasions. And it is true! It is really true. Jesus rose from the dead!"

I awakened at that moment to a bright new dawn, somehow back in my bed after soaring through two thousand years of Earth-time. I had fallen asleep the night before with a prayer on my lips that Jesus would help me with my doubts, fears, and unbelief. But I will never believe that all this was simply a dream created to answer my prayer. I know that I was somehow privileged to witness the eternal joy of the empty tomb of Jesus in some eternally timeless dimension of reality so that my doubts would henceforth be forever banished.

Jesus Appeared to Remove All Trace of Illness

"I've since come to accept the following experience as a dream," Laurie, a registered nurse from Maine, said somewhat reluctantly, "but for many years I truly believed that Jesus himself had appeared to me."

According to Laurie:

I was eight years old at the time of the incident. I had been feeling ill one night, so I retired early—which was very unusual for me. I did not tell either Mom or Dad of my condition, but I can remember lying in my bed wishing with all my might that I would soon feel better.

I suppose this is when I drifted off to sleep, but it all seemed so real when the image of Christ appeared at the foot of my bed. His arms were outstretched with his palms upward, and there was a glow all around Him and a look of such kindness and compassion in His eyes.

Almost at once I began feeling better, and I soon felt better than I could ever remember feeling. All tension and anxiety left me, and then I know that I truly drifted off to sleep. When I awakened the next morning, I felt completely well and energetic.

Healed During a Dream of Dining with Jesus

Kent, a successful architect from Oregon, said that he wouldn't begrudge anyone who wouldn't believe his story of how he was healed by Jesus in a dream.

"I must say that I find it pretty unbelievable myself," he admitted. "All I can say is that it happened."

Kent was reared in a Protestant tradition that accepts miracles and gifts of the Spirit, and he believes that Jesus can—and does—answer prayers and/or provide us with his loving mercies in our times of need.

Here is Kent's story:

In this extremely vivid and detailed dream, I saw myself in biblical times in a courtyard setting such as the one in which I would imagine the wedding at Cana would have taken place. You may remember that Jesus performed his first public miracle here when he turned water into wine. Anyway, I saw myself dressed in a blue and white robe, sitting on a bench at a long table that was loaded with all kinds of food and pitchers of wine. There were men and women dressed in colorful, elegant robes seated around me, laughing and talking, eating and drinking. Everyone seemed really festive and friendly.

And then I saw a handsome, distinguished young man approaching me, who I knew had to be a representation of Jesus as he would have appeared at the time of the wedding feast in Cana. He was wearing a white robe with a kind of red cape across his shoulders. He smiled at my table partners, indicating that he wished to sit next to me, and the couple nearest me obliged him by sliding over to make room for him to be seated at my right side.

"My Brother," he said in a voice of quiet authority, "I am happy to see you here among us at this festive occasion, but I am saddened to learn that you have not been well."

I was astonished that he knew of my physical complaints, but then, I reasoned, he is, after all, Jesus. He undoubtedly knew everything about me.

I explained to him that my doctor said that I had a very bad case of bleeding ulcers that had become so advanced that they would soon require surgery.

"You worry too much about too many things that are really beyond your control and are really not that important," he said. "Ever since you were a small boy you have fussed and fretted about the most inconsequential matters. It is one thing to be conscientious about the performance of one's responsibilities; it is quite another to be obsessed with the trivia associated with your work. You must learn to let go and to let God. You must trust in the Father to run the universe. If He cares about the number of feathers on a sparrow's wing, you must believe that He cares about you."

I agreed in essence with the words of Jesus, but I wondered how one ceased instantaneously to be the compulsive nitpicking worry-wart that I had always been. I also realized that the surgery would do me little good if I did not learn to control the nervous energy that had caused my upset stomachs, spastic colon, and bleeding ulcers.

As if Jesus had read my thoughts, he answered, "Nervous energy will become controlled, productive expression when you learn to trust that the Father is quite capable of running the universe without your assuming a prominent role in managing planet Earth."

The men and women at the table laughed and nodded their heads approvingly.

The man opposite me reached across the generous banquet feast and squeezed my hand, as if to offer his encouragement. I felt awkward when it occurred to me that the entire company at our table had been listening to the conversation that I had been having with Jesus.

"But first, before we repair your faith, my brother," Jesus said as he reached for a bowl of what appeared to be sliced fruits, nuts, and herbs, "let us heal your stomach."

I involuntarily shrank back as he handed me what appeared to be a slice of some kind of citrus fruit, perhaps a tangerine.

"I'm sorry," I apologized. "My doctor told me to avoid any kind of citrus fruits. Too much acid, you see."

The woman seated at my left assumed a face of disapproval and made a clucking sound with her tongue as if to scold me. "*Your doctor*? Dear Brother, you are in the company of the Master Physician, the greatest healer our world has ever known. Take the fruit that he offers you and stop being difficult. You should just be thankful that he has taken notice of your ills."

The heads of everyone at our table were nodding their agreement. Reluctantly, I accepted the slice of fruit and gingerly placed it in my mouth.

I was amazed at the texture, and at the sensation that it prompted from my taste buds. The fruit was somewhat pulpy, a bit tangy, but it made my mouth feel cool. It had kind of an apricot taste and feel, but there was also a touch of some kind of berry. And the soothing coolness of the mysterious fruit affected my throat when I swallowed it.

Jesus smiled, and our dinner companions applauded my compliance. I felt like a small boy being encouraged to eat all of his vegetables.

"And now the nuts," Jesus told me. "They have been coated with special herbs. Take a generous handful and eat them with great relish."

Once again I protested that my doctor had warned me against the ingesting of such harsh roughage as nuts and popcorn.

And once again the looks of astonishment from my fellow guests that I would dare question the

Great Healer forced me to place a handful of the mixture into my mouth without another word of objection or another thought of hesitation.

I know it was a dream, but I actually felt my teeth grinding and crunching the nuts and the herbs. And the taste was so unusual, like nothing that I have placed in my mouth before or since. A hint of black walnuts, perhaps a light dash of cashews, but the herbs transformed the nuts into a wondrous element far beyond the standard repertoire of my plebeian taste buds.

When Jesus handed me the cup of wine, I now knew better than to argue that my doctor had warned me that alcohol would really scorch my ulcers and have me vomiting fire.

"This is the wine that I have just changed from water for the benefit of our bridegroom," Jesus said. "Believe me, it is like no other wine that you have ever tasted. It is pure love and light distilled into the fruit of the vine that offers the strength of earth and sun."

I nodded as if I completely understood his words, and I emptied the cup without removing its rim from my lips.

As the wine filled my stomach, I experienced a divine fire sealing and healing my internal wounds. The touch of these flames was soothing and cool, and my entire body seemed to glow with their curative power.

"Trust in the Father," Jesus told me. "And be calm and at peace."

I awakened with those words echoing in my brain. It was 4:15 a.m.

My wife told me that I had been tossing and turning in my sleep, and she thoughtfully inquired if my ulcers were troubling me. "Do you want me to get your medicine for you, dear?"

I told her that I felt certain that my ulcers had been healed by Jesus in a dream and that I believed that I would never need my medicine ever again. She mumbled, "That's nice, dear," and fell back asleep.

But the next morning at breakfast, when I told her the dream in its entirety, she prayed with me that Jesus' healing of my ulcers would come true.

Two days later, at my regular appointment, my doctor confirmed that my condition was so greatly improved that surgery would no longer be necessary if I continued to get better.

Although he was clearly astonished by my sudden and dramatic improvement, he gave me a bunch of new prescriptions and encouraged me to "keep doing whatever I was doing."

I never got the prescriptions filled, and three weeks later, after an extensive examination, he enthusiastically agreed that I had been healed of my bleeding ulcers.

It was at that point that I told him about my dream of Jesus healing my ulcers at the wedding banquet, and he was diplomatic enough to say that there were many things that medical science could not explain. My wife and I will always believe that the Divine Physician did heal me in that vivid dream experience.

I have slowly learned to stop worrying about every "jot and tittle" as the Bible refers to minutia in one's life, and my new attitude of tranquility has prevented any recurrence of the ulcers.

An Early-Morning Jesus Encounter

Dr. Barry H. Downing has been a pastor at Northminster Presbyterian Church in Endwell, New York, for almost thirty years, and during that time he told us that he has heard an occasional story of a paranormal religious experience.

While Dr. Downing said that he had never heard a story in which anyone met Jesus and touched a physical body, he had heard one account in which a woman met Jesus in an early-morning dream or vision.

"The paranormal experiences of this woman before and after the Jesus encounter suggest that she was under the influence of a higher power," Dr. Downing said. "Her experience was not just something created by her own mind."

The following account, with our great appreciation, is Dr. Barry H. Downing's report of "An Early-Morning Jesus Encounter":

A woman, who goes by the name of Lynn, came to me to tell of her experience in part because her mother had been a member of my church for several years, and in part because of my interest in UFOs. I published my book, *The Bible and Flying Saucers,* in 1968, and have served as a theological adviser to the Mutual UFO Network for more than twenty years, as well as being a member of the national board of directors of the Fund for UFO Research. With this public reputation, I find people are willing to tell me stories they might not tell other pastors.

Lynn came to me in the spring of 1996, and wanted to talk about the paranormal dimensions of her life, dimensions that had a clear religious theme. Lynn is married, mother of a teenage son, and is a successful commercial artist. She is one of thirteen children, born of one mother.

From the time she was very young, she had visions or dreams of the future. On three successive nights she dreamed of the death of one of her sisters, warned the family, and the dream came true.

Although Lynn is not a church attender, she has a strong religious sense, and part of this religious/paranormal sense was that one day she would meet Jesus. She said that when she met Jesus, she planned to be very casual about it, to treat him as just a friend, not to go into some kind of "Wow, I can't believe it is you" type of response. The day before the vision, she had a sense it would happen soon.

In the spring of 1971, between 4 and 5 a.m., Lynn had the following encounter while she was asleep.

Lynn says, "Jesus was standing before me, about twelve feet away. I could not believe how tall he was. I am five feet, six inches tall, and he seemed to be at least six feet tall, which surprised me. He had his right hand raised about shoulder height, and he seemed to be making a sign with his hand. His mouth was not moving; he spoke to me with mental telepathy. I was walking up to him slowly. When I first saw him, I greeted him by saying, 'Hi, how's it going?' Although no one told me who it was, I knew it was Jesus. He had a smirk on his face, a Mona Lisa smile. He seemed to say, 'You are a cute girl, but I have serious business for you.' Suddenly, I found myself on all fours, my nose was right to the ground in a kneeling position, a position of worship."

This shocked Lynn, in light of her plan to greet Jesus casually when the encounter happened. Students of the Bible will not be shocked that she was "humbled" in this way. When Moses asked to see the face of God, God only allowed Moses to see his "back side" (Exodus 33). Moses had to be hidden in the "Rock of Ages," or he would die.

Lynn went on to say, "On the ground I could see his feet. He had beautiful feet, the skin tone was like a pale tan. I am an artist, and I thought it would be difficult to develop this skin tone in oil paints. I was taking a portrait oil painting class at this time, so painting skin tone was on my mind. While I was on the floor looking at his feet, I felt I was getting all kinds of messages, but I remember none of them. But I remember everything I said to Jesus."

When asked what Jesus looked like, Lynn said he had a full beard, and wore something like a white robe, although she thought it was whole cloth wrapped about him. The robe stopped just above his ankles, so she could see his bare feet clearly.

Lynn's bed faced a window, and when she awoke, she saw a crabapple tree outside that was in full bloom. The whole tree glittered, "as if there had been a heavy dew or rain, so that the whole tree sparkled. When I opened my eyes, I had a feeling of pure happiness and love. This was Jesus' way of saying to me, 'This was no dream.' "

Lynn said that the night after the Jesus Encounter, she went to bed hoping to see Jesus again. That did not happen. Instead, she had an involved dream about Clint Eastwood. In the dream she saw Clint with his wife and two blonde children. The next day the newspaper had a picture of Clint Eastwood, with his wife and children, exactly as they had appeared in the dream. Lynn believes this was a sign God gave to her so she would understand that her encounter with Jesus was real, and that she had been given spiritual gifts that would serve God's purpose.

In the Bible, divine encounters can either be physical experiences, or experiences that happen in a dream, or an altered state of consciousness. Examples of dreamlike encounters include Abram meeting God while in a "deep sleep" (Genesis 15), and Jacob dreaming the angels of God were climbing a ladder to heaven (Genesis 28).

At the same time, the "pillar of cloud and of fire" (Exodus 13:21, 22) was visible to the whole nation of Israel as Moses led them to the promised land. In the New Testament, Christians see Jesus as the physical presence of God. Jesus does make physical appearances to his disciples after his resurrection, and he lets them touch his body (John 20).

But after he ascends to heaven (Acts 1), I do not know of any direct physical contact between Jesus and humans.

The Eucharist, or Lord's Supper, becomes a ritual in the church by which Jesus is physically present. But when Stephen is stoned to death, he "sees Jesus" (Acts 7), but Stephen seems to be in an altered state of consciousness. The Apostle Paul likewise hears the voice of Jesus on the Damascus Road (Acts 9), but he does not seem to contact the physical body of Jesus.

What this might mean for us now as we think about modern persons who have an Encounter with Jesus I am not completely sure, but my impression is that Jesus, since his ascension, seems to be more likely to contact persons while they are in a deep sleep, or an altered state of consciousness, than to be physically present to them. Lynn's experience is consistent with that type of altered-state Encounter.

CHAPTER THREE

✠

Saved by Jesus' Amazing Grace

Amazing Grace, how sweet the sound that saved a wretch like me . . .

Gordon T., the well-dressed gentleman in his mid-fifties who joined us for dinner that night after our seminar, seemed to be the very image of propriety. It was difficult not to appear somewhat shocked when he made a startling confession:

At the age of twenty-one, I was more animal than human," he said. "I had been drinking for a mere five years, yet I was a completely warped personality. When I was seventeen, my conduct drove my family to have me removed from the home for the sake of the younger children.

> I joined one of the armed services, hoping that military discipline would help set me right. But violence had become my constant companion. Berserk escapades, blackouts, straitjackets, hospitals, jails, detention barracks became my principal environmental scene. Officially, during that brief period of time, I was charged and convicted a total of thirty-eight times for military and civilian infractions of the law.
>
> By the age of twenty, I was a social misfit who had abused every agency that had offered me assistance. Everyone who knew me regarded me as an unstable troublemaker.

Somewhere on his angry path to self-destruction, Gordon had attended a meeting of Alcoholics Anonymous.

"I could see it was a good program," he said with a smile, "for alcoholics. But, of course, I didn't consider myself in that category. Somewhere in their literature, though, I read the words, 'God as I understand Him' and 'Power greater than myself.' "

Gordon said that he had long since denied what he considered to be the impossible Christian platform of the orthodox churches.

"It simply didn't occur to me that these two simple expressions—'God as one understands Him' and 'recognizing a power greater than oneself'—offered the very spiritual and physical emancipation that I had so longingly pursued."

After that brief flirtation with A.A., Gordon yielded to the seductive siren call of the demon in the bottle and entered into a monthlong drunk.

"When I finally sobered up enough to recognize

my own face in the bathroom mirror, I was horrified by my ghastly reflection. I had the shakes and the entire room seemed to be pitching like a small boat on a stormy sea."

Gordon walked to a canal and strongly considered suicide. "Instead, thankfully, I called a man whom I had met during one of my few visits to an A.A. meeting.

> He came to my stinking, foul-smelling room and told me his own story of human degradation that almost made my fall from grace seem insignificant. The way that he told of accepting the love of Jesus to help support his journey on the path set forth by the A.A. began to move me.
>
> He told me how he had admitted his weakness and had cried out for the strength of the Lord Jesus to help support him. He had asked forgiveness for his awful sins. He had deserted his wife and three children. He had broken into homes and stolen objects to pawn. He had even robbed elderly men and women and children on the streets—all to support his miserable partnership with John Barleycorn. The love of Jesus had enabled him to put his wretched, wicked ways behind him and to enter the twelve-step program of A.A.

Gordon was greatly moved by the man's unmistakable depth of sincerity, and after his new friend had left, he sat up late into the night, reading verses from the Bible and passages from *The A.A. Way of Life* until he fell asleep.

He found himself fascinated by the revelation experience described by "Bill," the cofounder of Alcoholics Anonymous, as he lay in a hospital:

> My depression deepened unbearably, and finally it seemed as though I were at the very bottom of the pit . . . The last vestige of my proud obstinacy was crushed . . . I found myself crying out, "If there is a God, let Him show Himself! I am ready to do anything, anything!"
>
> Suddenly the room lit up with a great white light. It seemed to me . . . that I was on a mountain and that a wind not of air but of spirit was blowing. And then it burst upon me that I was a free man.
>
> Slowly the ecstasy subsided. I lay on the bed, but now for a time I was in another world, a new world of consciousness. All about me and through me there was a wonderful feeling of Presence, and I thought to myself, "So this is the God of the preachers!"

Gordon hadn't prayed since he was a boy, but that night he prayed that Jesus would fill him with His Holy Spirit and give him the strength to exorcise Demon Rum from his life forever.

He remembered a line or two of a prayer from his childhood, the one that he used to recite with his mother at bedtime: "Come into my heart, Lord Jesus . . . Cast out my sin and enter in . . . Be born in me this day."

Sometime during the night, Gordon experienced the first in a series of dramatic spiritual encounters. He told us that when he recounted his experience for others, as he was doing for us that evening, it was as if he could still feel the almost electric vibrations that seemed to fill his body and every corner of that dark, dismal room.

"I saw an illuminated vision of Jacob's ladder," he said. "At the base of the ladder, I witnessed a fierce death struggle between a dark-clad person and one clothed in white garments. It was a fight to the death—and I knew that both of the combatants were aspects of myself. Praise Jesus, the white-clad warrior was victorious—and the vision disappeared.

"I awakened shaking with joy and great excitement. I knew that freedom and a new life were now mine. I have not taken a drink since—and that was over thirty years ago.

"Think of it," Gordon emphasized as he concluded his moving account. "Years of slavery to alcohol were vanquished in one night after Jesus heard my prayer and gave me the strength to burst free of my dependence on the bottle."

CHAPTER FOUR

✠

Jesus Bestowed the Gifts of Spirit on a Shy Guy

Some years back, an American evangelist, who prefers to be known simply as "Reverend Bobby" for this account, told us how he had been given the courage and the ability to become a full-time laborer in Christ's earthly vineyard.

"When I was a kid in school," he began, "I was so shy and easily intimidated that I developed a temporary stutter. It was nearly impossible for me to speak up in class. I would blush and stammer and make a complete fool of myself. I would get so nervous worrying about whether or not I had to recite in class that sometimes I would throw up in the boys' room before I would take my seat."

The teenager's lack of self-confidence in the classroom led to his dropping out in his junior year of high school. He was eighteen and a good-sized boy, so he joined the Marine Corps, hoping to build his self-esteem.

"After coming out of the Marines, I worked in construction for a while, married, then went into the insurance business in Florida," he said. "My wife and I joined a church, and I received Jesus Christ as my savior. In a nine-month period, I enjoyed some of the richest blessings, revelations, and miraculous dealings of the Holy Spirit."

Reverend Bobby told how he was baptized "with the inner baptism of the Holy Ghost," a blessing that was consummated, or confirmed, by the experience of speaking in tongues, glossolalia.

"Shortly after I had spoken in tongues," he said, "I was involved in an act of miraculous healing. This kind of spiritual happening was brand new to me, and I probably would have scoffed at such an experience prior to my baptism by fire. This was probably the most instrumental event in the complete change of my life."

It was also at this time, Reverend Bobby recalled, that Jesus began to speak to him during his periods of prayer and meditation.

"He told me that he expected me to make a drastic change in my life. Jesus said that I was to preach His gospel. I was to go the way that he would lead me. In other words, I received my calling."

Reverend Bobby respected his divine commission from Jesus, but just the same, he felt great apprehension.

"I had never been able to do public speaking. I was intimidated by crowds. Just as when I was a kid, I would still get stage fright so bad that I would become ill. So when the Lord said that He wanted me to preach, I thought surely that He must be making a big mistake."

But in his hours of earnest prayer, Reverend Bobby told his Lord that if that was what He willed, then he would have to depend on Him for the power to do so.

> I also confessed that I had never been much of a Bible reader, but Jesus assured me that through the power of the Holy Spirit, the Word of God would be open to me.
>
> Jesus told me that I would be able to understand all the hidden meanings in His parables. I would perceive various allegories and be given everything that I would need to know to be an effective preacher.

Reverend Bobby had a conversation with the state secretary of his Christian denomination. "He told me that the only real way to be sure of my call from Jesus was to get up there and try preaching to folks." Reverend Bobby agreed with the church administrator, but he said that he would need at least a month to prepare.

"The church committee gave me two weeks! They said that I would lead the worship and give the sermon in two weeks!"

At first, he was terrified. "But I just opened the Bible, let it fall where it may, and let the Lord Jesus speak to me. As He spoke to me, I took notes—and from there I composed a sermon. I put it on tape, played it back once, and forgot about it."

When the appointed Sunday arrived, Reverend Bobby fully expected to be nervous and to conduct his usual struggle with the butterflies in his stomach.

> But when I stepped into the pulpit, it was as if I had been born for preaching. I just opened my mouth and let the Lord Jesus talk through me.
>
> Let me say that this church had not had anyone come forward to dedicate his life to Jesus or to make a first-time commitment or acceptance of Christ in about six months. I daresay that in a period of six years, that church had only had five or six people come forward.
>
> But the Holy Spirit took over and spoke through me—and at the end of the sermon, fifty-four people came forward either to rededicate their lives to Christ or to accept Him for the first time."

Reverend Bobby accepted a call to a church and left his job with the insurance company.

It took a good deal of courage to make the decision and to take such a great cut in salary—but the courage came through the Holy Spirit!" he said.

"My former mundane existence has been changed into a vital, very meaningful, and very rich life," Reverend Bobby said, concluding the account of his spiritual transformation.

"I have received a realization of God and of His will—and some of the revelations that I have received have been astounding!"

CHAPTER FIVE

✠

Prayers to Jesus Protected Her from a Raging Inferno

Thirty-year-old Anna Gallo, who lives in the Detroit area, has always been an extremely religious person. Each night at bedtime she joins hands with her children—Cathie, Susie, and Ben—to say their "goodnight" prayers to Lord Jesus aloud together.

"And every night before I go to my own bed with my husband, I always pray that Jesus and the angels will protect our home from all evil and all harm—especially from fire," Anna said.

When she was just a girl of nine, Anna's aunt lost her beautiful home to a terrible fire that also left the woman horribly burned and scarred. Since that time, Anna has had an overwhelming fear of fire.

Then, one spring night in May of 1994, Anna had just returned from the neighborhood supermarket when she began to smell smoke.

"Cathie, Susie, and I were putting away the groceries when I detected the acrid scent of smoke," she recalled. "At first I was afraid that it was our house that was on fire, and I prayed to Jesus to deliver us from harm."

She searched through their home, looking in every room for any sign of fire. When she couldn't find any source for the smoke in her own home, Anna stepped outside.

"I was horrified when I saw smoke and flames coming from the Pendells' home, just a few doors away," she said.

She knew that a family of four lived in the house with the wife's elderly parents, the Worsleys. She glanced around the front yard and saw that other neighbors were helping George Pendell and his two kids from the house. Some of them looked as though they were in bad shape from smoke inhalation. Anna knew that Linda Pendell worked nights, so at first it appeared as though everyone was present and accounted for.

But then one of the Pendell Children started coughing violently and waving his arms wildly. "Grand . . . pa, Grandma . . . still upstairs!"

George Pendell had collapsed on the sidewalk, but he tried to get back to his feet. "Dear God," he cried, "my wife's parents are still in their upstairs bedroom."

The flames were spewing from every opening, and great black billows of smoke rose skyward. The house was now a raging inferno.

Anna heard someone near her say, "It's awful.

Those old folks are trapped up there. Too late to save them now."

And then she heard another voice speaking directly to her: *"Anna, you must save those people. You must enter the flames. It is up to you!"*

Anna's knees felt weak and her heart pounded at her chest. How could she of all people walk into that blazing furnace? She had had a fear of fire since she was a child.

And then she thought of the Hebrew children thrown into the fiery furnace and how the Lord had kept them safe and untouched by the flames.

At the same time, she felt some kind of force drawing her toward the bright orange flames that curled around the rear of the house and snaked up to the second floor.

She remembered praying, "Lord, thy will be done!" And then she felt the force continuing to pull her, frightened and trembling, into the burning house.

"It must have been the hand of Jesus that moved me up a flight of stairs that was totally obscured by thick, black, suffocating smoke," Anna said. "Somehow I sensed that the fire had started in the kitchen, perhaps when grease caught fire and ignited the cupboards above the stove."

She was nearly to the top of the stairs when she gagged and choked on the thick smoke that rolled around her. She gasped for air, and her survival reflexes demanded that she turn back.

But the voice was insistent: *"You must go on, Anna. The lives of two people depend on you."*

Once again she could feel the force moving her up the stairs. She began to cough as the smoke filled her lungs and stung her eyes.

"Cover your face with your jacket!" The voice told her.

Anna did as the voice advised her, and she finally reached the room where she could see the elderly man and woman lying on the bed.

"I thought they were already dead from smoke inhalation, because they lay so very still—but amazingly, they were only sleeping soundly!" Anna said.

She shook the couple awake and shouted, "Fire! Fire! We've got to get out of here—or we're all going to die!"

She helped them get to their feet and ushered them to the stairs. Within a few minutes, all three of them had stumbled outside to safety.

By that time, the fire truck had arrived, along with its crew of professional firefighters. Anna was more than happy to relinquish the task of extinguishing the flames to their expertise. She had done all that the voice had asked her to do.

The neighbors were quick to declare that Anna had put her life on the line to save the elderly members of the Pendell family. An investigator from the fire department later called her a true hero.

Anna only shrugged and accepted her neighbors' thanks graciously. In her mind, she knew that the Lord Jesus to whom she prayed each night to deliver her and hers from evil and to keep fire away from their home had chosen her to act on His behalf. It was her firm and unshakable belief that it had been Jesus' will that she help her elderly neighbors when they were threatened by flames of destruction and death.

"And Jesus and his angels stayed with me amidst the flames to keep me safe from harm," she said.

CHAPTER SIX

✠

Encountering Jesus on the Interstates

The accounts are all basically the same with few variations:

A couple driving across America on vacation spot a long-haired, bearded hitchhiker standing at the side of the road. Although he appears somewhat disheveled and his clothes are a bit ragged, they decide to take a chance that he is not a serial murderer and pick him up.

After they have driven for a few miles, the hitcher, in answer to their inquiries regarding his destination, begins to speak of Heaven and the unseen world. His words touch their hearts and the relieved couple realize that they have made a safe decision and have picked up a very spiritual fellow.

The hitcher then shifts his comments to issue a

number of warnings concerning the day of judgment that will soon be at hand for all of humankind and the entire world. The backseat becomes a makeshift pulpit as he advises the couple that "Jesus will return soon. The Second Coming of Christ is at hand. Prepare ye for the day of the Lord."

At this point in the narrative, the story has two equally popular endings:

1) The couple looks around and discovers to their astonishment that their passenger has disappeared. They then realize that the man was Jesus, warning them to prepare for the coming Judgment Day.

2) Just before he disappears before their astonished eyes, the holy hitchhiker reveals himself to be Jesus, who leaves them with a blessing and a final warning to be prepared.

The above account—which has been told to us at least a dozen times as an actual event that happened to a friend of a friend of the storyteller—seems to us to be a variation of the urban legend of the phantom hitchhiker. [A driver picks up a lovely young woman who asks to be taken home. Almost as he arrives at the requested destination, she disappears. Puzzled, he knocks at the door of the house and is shown a photograph of the same young woman—who was killed several years ago trying to get home.]

Now blend the old story of the phantom hitchhiker with the biblical account of the appearance of the newly risen Jesus to the two disciples on the road to Emmaus. [The afternoon after his resurrection, Jesus appeared to Cleopas and another disciple as they walked on the road to Emmaus, about seven miles northwest of Jerusalem.] It seems that we might have discovered the two original sources that were combined to fashion the tale of the contemporary hitchhiking Jesus.

We were quite surprised not long ago when a fervent born-again Christian, who normally rejects all accounts of contemporary revelation, told us the story of the hitchhiking Jesus vanishing in a couple's backseat and swore that it was true. The account was circulating among members of his church, he said, and it was being repeated by "folks who would never lie."

We gently tried to explain that the tale appeared to be a variation on a classic urban legend, combined with the gospel account of the risen Christ appearing to two disciples on the road, but we received a very indignant argument in return.

"We are approaching the End Times, Armageddon, the last great battle between the forces of Good and Evil, when Christ shall return in the skies with legions of angels to send Satan back into the pit and to conduct his judgment on all of humankind," we were solemnly reminded. "It seems to be in the order of things that Jesus could return in disguise and then reveal himself to certain individuals so that they might be prepared for the opportunity of the Rapture, which will deliver all true believers from the planet."

Of course, neither must we be dogmatic in such a wondrous and mysterious arena of human experience as the claimed manifestations of Christ. We must surely concede that all things are possible for such a powerful, supernatural being, for the following stories of a hitchhiking Jesus, although quite different from the accounts of a disappearing backseat preacher of Judgment Day, were told to us with earnest conviction.

The "Hippie Hitchhiker" Stopped a Heart Attack

Wayne Fiske, fifty-eight, has been a cross-country trucker for over thirty years, driving for a number of major trucking firms.

"I'll always remember that cold December night in 1988," he wrote in his account of the remarkable experience. "My older brother Eddie was riding with me on that job, more or less to keep me company, and also to hitch a ride to his daughter's home in Aberdeen, South Dakota."

Wayne said that it was good to have a chance to talk with Eddie and to catch up on events both major and minor in their lives.

"Eddie is four years older than me, fifty-seven at that time. Although we had a sister born after me, I would always be the kid in the family to him. To his way of thinking, I had probably had only two or three ideas in my whole life that he didn't think were stupid or off the wall."

In spite of an older brother's disdain for a younger brother's reasoning processes, Wayne said that the two men got along fairly well.

> Our biggest conflict was over religion. While I continued to raise my family in the Methodist traditions of our parents, Eddie thought church-going and Bible reading were bunk.
>
> His trouble was that he was just a kid when he had enlisted in the Marines during the Korean

"police action," and he had brought our small-town Nebraska innocence along with him into the tough outside world. The things he saw during service overseas had so shocked his unprepared sensibilities that he had returned home a virtual atheist, and we used to get into some pretty loud arguments over religion.

Wayne remembered stopping at a small roadside diner to tank up on coffee and cheeseburgers before they hit a long stretch of desolate highway.

"We got into another argument over our food when I gently—I thought—suggested that Eddie start watching his weight. He was at least forty pounds overweight, and I knew that he had started to drink hard liquor pretty steadily. Plus he smoked two to three packs of cigarettes a day. None of those things are good for the old ticker, and I reminded Eddie that Dad had died of a heart attack when he was about his age."

Shortly after they had returned to the truck and had traveled a few miles down the road, they spotted a hitchhiker at the side of the highway.

"Although company policy is strong against hitch-hikers, I wanted to pick the guy up," Wayne said. "It was well below zero out there, and the hitcher barely had any clothes on—I mean a light jacket, that was all. I figured he would freeze to death. And since there were two of us in case he should try any monkey business, I thought I should stop and pick him up."

Eddie raised no real objections. After all, he too was a passenger, and Wayne was the captain of the ship. But he stated firmly that the hitcher had better not mind his heavy smoking.

"The man looked to be about thirty-five," Wayne recalled. "His long hair looked clean and his beard was well groomed, so I felt better about that. I mean, he wasn't a dirty bum or anything. Probably just a guy down on his luck.

"The most noticeable thing about him was his eyes. You almost couldn't help staring at them. But you know, I can't remember what color they were. What was important, though, was that they were really kind and expressive eyes that made you feel friendly toward him right away."

But to Wayne's discomfort and annoyance, Eddie didn't seem to feel the friendliness and kindness emanating from the man, and he started picking on the hitchhiker as soon as he was seated in the cab.

> Right away he asked him if he had been in the service, and when the hitcher said he hadn't, Eddie began to rail against peaceniks and beatniks and bums. He made it sound like the guy must be all three and that to be all of those things was something like being a child molester, a dope addict, and a traitor rolled into one.
>
> The hitcher, though, was unruffled, and very soft spoken in his answers. I could see that the guy's quiet voice was only making Eddie all the more ticked off against life in general and the stranger in particular.

Eddie was shouting something about the alleged evils of welfare programs and food stamps when he suddenly clutched at his chest and emitted a terrible, gasping cry.

> I knew right away that he was having a heart attack, and I really started to panic. It was about two o'clock in the morning, and we were miles and miles away from any hospital. I pulled over as quickly and as safely as I could, and I started to pray out loud to God to help Eddie.
>
> And that's when the hitcher does this incredible thing. He reached out for Eddie's chest and lay his open palm against it. 'Be healed,' he said in his soft way of speaking. Right away Eddie stops moaning, and it is immediately obvious that he is feeling a whole lot better.
>
> And then the hitchhiker started to glow. I swear, there was a beautiful bluish-white light that seemed to emanate from his very being, all around his body. The entire cab of the truck was filled with that incredible light.

Eddie began to breathe easier, and Wayne could tell that his brother was truly healed, just as the mysterious stranger had commanded.

> He had our complete attention at that point. We knew that this was no common hitchhiker. This guy was from another world.
>
> He talked to us for a long time after that. How long, I don't know. It was as if we were somehow in-between ordinary time. He knew everything about Eddie and me and our families. It was incredible. Neither Eddie nor me said a word. We just listened.

Wayne remembered that the man went on to talk of revelations of the future and about the coming time of judgment and renewal for all of humankind.

"I remember that he quoted a lot of scripture. And then he disappeared. I mean, he was just gone. Like that. In the twinkling of an eye."

Wayne remains convinced that the mysterious hitchhiker was Jesus.

> Or an angel, anyway. Needless to say, Eddie changed his attitude toward religion and nearly everything else that night. Really, the experience became a turning point in both our lives. Now we know for sure it is true what others have to accept on faith.
>
> We don't care what anyone else says or thinks about our experience that night. We know that it really happened. Our families believed us. That's all that matters to us.
>
> Maybe some others will believe that Jesus is really alive and somehow always with them when they hear us tell our story. It's up to them. It really is just as Jesus said, all matters of the heart and soul are up to the individual.

Jesus Saved Him from a Fiery Car Crash

Twenty-eight-year-old salesman Charles Groff of Vermont was returning home after two weeks of "dismal motel rooms and disinterested retailers" when he fell asleep at the wheel while driving on a lonely rural road.

"My '95 Taurus slammed into a concrete bridge abutment, then caromed down a ditch, rolling over twice before it flipped over on its top," Groff said.

Charles was unconscious for an undetermined length of time, and when he once again became aware of his surroundings, he realized that he was hanging upside down by his seat belt.

"The windshield was shattered, and I slowly became aware that the gritty substance in my mouth was bits of glass. My eyes were also trying to blink away tiny pieces of glass."

Charles was comforted to know that he wasn't dead, but he began to panic when it occurred to him that he didn't really know how much longer he might be alive.

"Although I could find the release button of the seat belt, for some reason it didn't work. I don't know if it was the weight of my body that prevented me from unbuckling the seat belt or what, but I seemed to be stuck there, dangling like a fish on the end of a line.

"And I was certain I could smell gasoline. I had an image of the car exploding and me burning to death."

He had a frightening thought of the world without him. "I knew that the United Nations and the stock market could get along without me, but I thought of my wife Maryann and my two kids, Keith and Kathy, our three-year-old twins. I wanted to be around to watch them grow up, to attend college, to get married."

Charles felt tears sting his eyes, and he began to pray for help. He acknowledged that he had been no saint during his years on the road. He had begun to drink heavily to kill the nights of loneliness and boredom, and he had also begun to extend certain barroom flirtations into one-night stands. One of his dalliances had even turned into an affair that had lasted for several months.

"The headlights were smashed and dead, but the

dash lights were still on. I caught a glimpse of my bloody face in the reflection of the windshield and cried out loud in anguish."

And then he heard the sound of footsteps in the gravel outside his crippled and overturned Taurus.

"I heard this voice say that I had to get out of there fast. I answered that I had no argument there, but I couldn't get free. Immediately, this man was stretching his arms inside to help me. With one hand, he undid the release button on the seat belt. With the other, he helped me drop free without landing so hard that I would be injured."

Charles could not help noticing how strong the man was as he assisted him to move across the ceiling of the upside-down car and make his way out of the damaged vehicle.

"My rescuer turned out to be a rather slender, but well built, man of medium height. He had long, shoulder-length hair and a beard. His voice was very soft and warm. For the life of me, I just can't remember how he was dressed. What I remember most about him was his soulful eyes."

The man's strong arms helped Charles out of the ditch and away from the crash site. "We must move away from the car," the stranger told him.

"I don't imagine that we had walked thirty feet when the car burst into flames. I shuddered and gasped when I thought how close I had come to being consumed by the fire that was now blazing from one end of my Taurus to the other."

Charles could feel that he was badly shaken and was cut and bleeding from numerous scratches, but all in all, he seemed all right. After all, he was walking away from the scene of the crash unassisted.

"There's a farmhouse with a good family not more

than a hundred yards away," the stranger told him. "You'll be all right now."

And then as Charles turned to thank him and to ask his name, the man answered, "I am the Light of the world. I am giving you a second chance, Charles. Take full advantage of the opportunity. Change your ways and learn to appreciate all the wonders and miracles that God has given you."

Before Charles's astonished eyes, the man was suddenly transformed into a brilliant light.

"It was the brightest light that I have ever seen. It became so blinding that I fell to the asphalt of the road and covered my eyes.

"When I looked up again after a few moments, the light and my rescuer had disappeared. There was no trace of the being that I then knew with all my heart was Jesus Christ."

Charles remains convinced that it was truly Jesus of Nazareth who came to deliver him from certain death that evening.

"I became a changed man. I quit the road and took a job in my hometown so I could be home with my family every night. I stopped heavy drinking, and I have remained totally faithful to my wife ever since that night. I want to be as clean and sober and as sinless as I can be the next time that I meet my Lord Jesus face to face."

A Message and a Miracle from a Mysterious Hitchhiker

The experience of Catherine and John Bioletto of Los Angeles is much more similar to the earlier examples that we provided of the classic Vanishing

Jesus Hitchhiker stories, but it has the added element of a miracle that was performed for the couple.

In December of 1994, Catherine and John were driving to Lake Tahoe, Nevada, on a holiday vacation, when they spotted a long-haired, bearded hitcher at the side of the road.

"Don't stop for him," warned fifty-five-year-old Catherine. "He's poorly dressed. Probably some drug addict who'll try to rob us. Remember all the warnings about the hazards of picking up a hitchhiker. Just keep going!"

John, two months away from his sixtieth birthday, chuckled at his wife's concern. He read the papers and watched television news, too, but this guy didn't look like a junkie or a hardcase to him.

"You want your hitchhikers to wear three-piece suits?" he teased Catherine. "It's cold out there. Let's give the guy a break."

As they were slowing to a stop, John did work out a compromise with his wife's apprehensions. They would let the hitcher get in the front seat and Catherine would climb into the back. If the man did try anything funny, she would spray him with the mace that she always carried in her purse.

"As the young man got into our car, I calmed my fears," Catherine told us in her account of the incident. "He had the most beautiful eyes, and there was a wonderful aura of peace around him. It didn't matter that his clothes were worn and tattered and that his hair was long and kind of straggly. His quiet manner told you that he could be trusted.

"But soon after he was seated in the front and I was settled in the backseat, I began to suspect that John had had an ulterior motive in stopping for the man. Almost right away, John started picking on him for being an out-of-work transient."

For three or four minutes the young man sat in silence while John presented an unsolicited catalog of his apparent faults.

"Look at you," John scolded. "A healthy, strapping young guy. How old are you? Thirty-four, thirty-five? When I was your age, I had served in the military, graduated from college, and had a good job, a wife, and two kids. Have you no self-respect? A bum, that's what you are. A ragged, tattered bum, just wandering around the countryside without assuming any responsibilities."

Finally the hitcher answered in a soft, pleasant voice: "Judge not that ye be not judged."

At this point Catherine told us that she feared they had picked up some religious fanatic, for the soft-spoken stranger continued to quote numerous passages from scripture that cautioned against one's judging one's fellow human.

"But then he began to speak of personal matters and some rather shameful incidents from John's past. He referred to details in our married life that no one, not even our children, could have known," Catherine said. "Finally he got to some extremely intimate situations that made me start to cry. John's mouth dropped open and his eyes bulged. He asked the young man who he was and how he could know so much about us."

The hitchhiker did not identify himself just then, but he began to speak of a coming time of a great cleansing of the Earth and of a season of judgment for all humankind.

"Time seemed to stand still," Catherine said, "but he probably spoke to us of the End Times for half an hour or so. He told us that we must begin to prepare for difficult times ahead and that we must begin to 'set our house in order' and to be certain that our souls were clean and without blame or blemish."

When Catherine once again began to notice their actual physical environment, she saw to her great concern that they had been caught by a blizzard and were driving on a snow-packed mountain highway near Lake Tahoe.

"At about the same time that we were emerging from the stranger's mesmerizing talk of omens and portents to come, John shouted that our automobile's electrical system had suddenly malfunctioned. Our lights, wipers, heater, and windows no longer worked. Without the wipers and the defroster to keep it clear, the windshield soon became a white wall of snow and ice and it was impossible for John to see where he was driving."

John managed to pull their car safely off the road and on to the shoulder without getting stuck in a snow drift.

"We're really in a jam," he said. "We have no headlights or taillights to warn approaching vehicles that we're stranded here. Someone could easily swerve on the slick highway and run into us before they see us. We have no heat to keep us from freezing to death, and it's too far to walk to the next town."

Catherine said that was when the stranger revealed his true presence.

"I am the Light of the world," he said. "If you believe in me and in my truth, you shall be saved. I have issued you many warnings this day. Share them with others, so that many will be prepared for my Second Coming."

After he had spoken these words, he stretched out his left arm and held his open palm just a few inches from the dashboard.

"A brilliant blue-white light like a bolt of electricity shot forth from the palm of his hand and struck the dashboard," Catherine said. "The light it made was blinding, and it filled the entire automobile. In that same instant, the hitchhiker disappeared right before our eyes. And in the next instant, the lights, wipers, heater, defroster, windows—everything—started working again all at once."

Catherine and John Bioletto were able to drive safely the remainder of the distance to Lake Tahoe.

"During the drive to our hotel, neither one of us spoke more than two words," Catherine said. "Since that time, though, we have discussed the marvelous experience over and over again. And we have shared it with many, many people, just as the mysterious hitchhiker told us to do."

And just what did they believe was the hitchhiker's true identity?"

"It could have been an angel of the Lord, I suppose," Catherine said. "But the way in which he said that *he* was the Light of the world and to believe in him and in his truth, we just have to believe that it was Jesus himself."

CHAPTER SEVEN

✠

Does the Shroud of Turin Depict the True Image of Jesus?

In the fall of 1978, the ancient Shroud of Turin was exhibited publicly for the first time since 1933, thus refueling anew the fires of controversy that have raged intermittently since the first century C.E.

Is this cloth the authentic burial shroud of Jesus? Is the image impressed on its coarse fibers the actual physical representation of Jesus of Nazareth as he lay in the tomb after his cruel death by crucifixion at the hands of Roman soldiers? When we look at the shroud, are we seeing a kind of photograph of Jesus that can accurately depict his actual human appearance?

The fourteen-by-four-foot shroud has been kept

under guard in a Roman Catholic chapel in Turin, Italy since 1452, and it was previously examined by technical investigators in 1973. Although they were unable to date it with certainty, scientists at the Los Alamos Scientific Laboratory in New Mexico announced that the burial cloth appeared to be authentic, woven of a type of linen typically used in Jewish burials in the Holy Land about 30 C.E., thus approximating the date of Jesus' crucifixion.

As for the remarkable image imprinted on the shroud, Ray Rogers, a physical chemist of the Los Alamos design engineering division, stated his opinion that the impression was formed by "a burst of radiant energy—light, if you like."

Such a view is in harmony with gospel references to a brilliant light from heaven and the process of transformation undergone by Jesus at the moment of his resurrection on Easter Sunday after three days in the tomb.

A statement issued by the Los Alamos Laboratory, operated by the University of California for the U.S. Department of Energy, explains one hypothesis that draws a parallel "between the mysterious images on the shroud and the fact that images were formed on stones by fireball radiation from the atomic bomb at Hiroshima."

Most of the experts who have examined the Shroud of Turin have agreed that the image was not painted on the cloth, for the mysterious portrait is not absorbed into the fibers. Neither could the image have been placed on the shroud by any ordinary application of heat or the fibers would have been scorched.

The gospel accounts of the crucifixion state that Jesus was whipped and beaten unmercifully by

Roman soldiers, who contemptuously placed a cruel crown of thorns on the head of the man who was identified as the "King of the Jews."

The brutal humiliation completed, Jesus was marched through the streets of Jerusalem bearing the wooden cross on his back before he was nailed to its horizontal bar at the place of execution. After his apparent death, a spear was thrust into his side by a Roman soldier.

Researchers have declared the front and back images on the Shroud of Turin to be anatomically correct if the cloth had been used to wrap a crucified man in its folds. The impressions are of a tall man with a bearded, majestic countenance, his hands crossed with the imprints of nails through the wrists and feet. The right side of the man's chest was pierced.

In addition, the image is said by investigators to bear the marks of whip lashes on the back. The man's right shoulder is chafed, as if from having borne a rough, heavy object. A number of puncture wounds appear around the head, and one cheek displays a pronounced bruise. The chest cavity is expanded, as if the victim were trying desperately to draw air into the lungs, a common occurrence and a typical physical response during crucifixion.

Since 1978, the Shroud of Turin has been hailed as physical proof of Jesus' resurrection from the dead and his triumph over the grave—or condemned as a hoax crafted by medieval monks who sought to create the ultimate holy relic for pilgrims to venerate.

Los Alamos chemist Ray Rogers is one of a number of scientists who believes that the burial cloth is truly the shroud of Jesus Christ. In his view—and in that of many others—the Shroud of Turin answers the eternal question of whether humans can achieve immortality:

> If Christ was resurrected from the dead, then the gospels are truth, and eternal life—immortality—is offered to all of us. What better way, if you were a deity, of regenerating faith in a skeptical age than to leave evidence 2,000 years ago that could be defined only by the technology available in that skeptical age? ["Scientists see energy in shroud's 'Christ' image," Associated Press, March 26, 1978]

APPARITIONS OF JESUS THAT RESEMBLE THE SHROUD OF TURIN IMAGE

Since 1973, we have been privileged to number among our dearest friends Frank C. Tribbe, editor of *Spiritual Frontiers,* the journal of Spiritual Frontiers Fellowship International and author of *Portrait of Jesus?: The Illustrated Story of the Shroud of Turin,* who has been researching the mystery of the shroud for over twenty-five years.

In an article that he prepared for the *Journal* [Winter/Spring 1993], Frank wrote of the fascinating, "Apparitions of Jesus that Mimic the Shroud of Turin Image."

In 1972, Frank and his wife attended a slide-lecture on the Shroud of Turin by the late Colonel Frank O. Adams and saw for the first time the image of the man of the shroud, as well as Phoenix artist Ris Phillips's portrait based on the shroud face, which had been commissioned by Adams. Frank purchased Adams's book and a set of his slides, and his wife Audre acquired a life-sized color print of the Phillips portrait.

A year earlier, the Tribbes' friend, Virginia S. of the Washington, D.C., area, had told them of an experience with Jesus in a home in Myrtle Beach, South Carolina, where she had been visiting. She had gone there at an arranged time expressly because her hostess felt that she should make the acquaintance of a local lady:

> And indeed when the two met there was an "electricity" between them. In fact, they sat . . . and talked for so long that the hostess excused herself and went to bed. Suddenly, Virginia "saw Jesus" standing in the room.
>
> Not knowing how her new friend might react to such an idea, Virginia just stared and said nothing. Following Virginia's gaze, the lady looked in the same direction, and after a moment asked, "Virginia, do you see anything there?"
>
> Then, each described what she was seeing, and their descriptions of the "being" matched perfectly—and they both knew it was Jesus! And the apparition's appearance to them that night had a profound effect on both ladies' lives.

After they had attended the shroud lecture, Audre asked their friend Virginia to come by the Tribbes' apartment without giving any hint of the reason. The unframed print of the Ris Phillips portrait hung temporarily on a closet door, facing the front door.

The moment Virginia entered the apartment, she

saw the portrait of Jesus and grabbed Audre's arm, saying, "That's Him. That's Him!"

Virginia rushed over to the portrait, then added: "Remember, I told you He didn't smile or have any expression, but we felt such love! And this portrait conveys the same feeling."

Virginia paused, put out her hand to touch the image of Jesus. "Oh, Audre," she exclaimed, "feel the heat coming from Him!"

Frank writes that while Audre did experience the sensation of heat that Virginia reported, she silently wondered if the closet door might not be warm for some other reason. However, checking the next day, "Audre found that the closet door was normal and cool, but she still felt heat from the portrait, and since then has felt the heat from it on other occasions."

When the Tribbes inquired of Colonel Adams regarding the experience, he quickly informed them that many people had reported feeling heat or some sort of "spiritual energy" emanating from other prints of the portrait.

Encountering Jesus on the Stairway of a Bavarian Castle

Another instance Frank shares in his article concerns the experience of twenty-four-year-old Susan B., who, in 1976 and 1977, was living in a beautiful Bavarian castle while working with an interdenominational religious group, "Youth with a Mission," in a small farming village in Germany's Black Forest area, some sixty miles from Munich:

> Late one night, and very tired, Susan started up the castle's winding stairway to get ready for bed.

> The long climb seemed a formidable obstacle for a girl with the handicap of cerebral palsy. But, although she still hoped for a physical healing, she proceeded to thank the Lord for giving her strength for each step. After four or five steps, she felt a tingle go from the top of her head down to her toes; she stopped and looked up. There, on the stairs ahead of her, stood Jesus.
>
> She just "knew" it was Him . . . the love she saw in His eyes was absolutely overwhelming to her . . . "to see this love, face to face, is indescribable . . . it felt as if darts were piercing my heart." [Jesus] said nothing orally, but stood with hands held out to her.
>
> Susan describes the apparition of Jesus as being very tall, looking "big" and "magnified." He was wearing a white robe with gold overtones; his hair and full beard were dark brown, as were his eyes; his skin was olive-toned and he had a prominent nose; his face seemed "long," definitely not round or oval-shaped. She could not seem to speak but the love in His eyes said a lot to her. After about a minute, He faded away, and Susan began to laugh and cry.

Some two years later, when she first saw reproductions of the shroud face in a newspaper article, Susan B. knew immediately and with certainty that it was the face of the apparition of Jesus that appeared to her on the stairs in a German castle.

The experience didn't bring Susan a healing of her cerebral palsy, but she feels that it did bring her a healing of the emotions and has brought her true peace.

"Such experiences may have little vicarious evidence for others," Frank writes, "but if it happens to you, *you know.*"

Frank Tribbe's Exciting "Shroud of Turin Update"

In a letter dated August 13, 1996, Frank expressed his excitement that Pope John Paul II has authorized public exhibitions of the shroud in the springs of 1998 and 2000. "Recent research makes the likelihood greater than ever that the shroud image is the Resurrection likeness of Jesus," he told us.

Herewith we are pleased to present the text of *A Shroud of Turin Update* by Frank C. Tribbe, a paper that was read in September 1996 *in absentia* by Canon Michael Perry at the Annual Conference of Churches' Fellowship for Psychical and Spiritual Studies in London, England:

> As recently as 1975 very few people recognized or had significant knowledge concerning the name, "Shroud of Turin." Even among Roman Catholic Church members and clergy, a negligible number knew any details except that such an item did exist as a sacred relic.
>
> In 1978 two events altered the public's general knowledge. First, was the release by Doubleday publishers of the excellent book, *The Shroud of Turin: The Burial Cloth of Jesus Christ?* by Ian Wilson, late of Bristol, England. The second event was the September/October exhibition of the Shroud in Turin, with viewing by three and a half million

people, followed by a Sindonological Congress of experts on October 7 and 8; and following immediately thereafter, October 8 to 13, was a detailed, round-the-clock, 120-hour, scientific examination of the Shroud that included more than 30,000 photographs of various kinds. The latter effort was primarily by scientists from the United States who had brought 72 crates of equipment weighing eight tons.

The significance of Wilson's book cannot be over-emphasized. For the first time, readers of English, world-wide, were given a clear and complete account of the history of this mysterious cloth. Even more importantly, Wilson presented the results of his historical research which brought continuity, from A.D. 33 to 1204, to the story of the Shroud and its travels; his conclusions that the Shroud of Jesus, the Face of Edessa, and the Mandylion of Constantinople were all the same relic has not been seriously challenged to this day. He also postulated, without data, a "Knights Templar connection" for the so-called "missing years" of 1204 to 1357, which has recently been slightly modified by discovery of additional records (as presented by historian Daniel C. Scavone of the University of Southern Indiana), that show the Shroud's presence in Athens and Besancon (France) during that period; the extensive copying of the Shroud Face, by or on behalf of the Knights Templars at the Besancon Church, indirectly led to the public's apparent acceptance of heresy charges against the Templars—which in turn led to Papal revocation of their charter, plus conviction and execution of their leaders by the French ecclesiastical court, as Wilson detailed it. The Templar involvement, as thus modified, was further validated by Wilson and others when a matching Shroud face was found behind the false ceiling of an outbuilding in Templecombe, southern England, on premises that had once been a Templar recruitment and training center.

My own book in 1983 (*Portrait of Jesus?—The Illustrated Story of the Shroud of Turin*) attempted to summarize the entire Shroud story for the general reader, with especial attention to the detailed scientific findings of the preceding fifteen years. And it is particularly noteworthy that of the multinational mix of scientists curious about the Shroud, who included atheists, Jews, Protestants and Catholics, none of the original hands-on group has ever made an adverse comment about its authenticity. Moreover, their nearly fifty multi-disciplinary and peer-reviewed reports have disclosed many new mysteries but in no respect have they questioned a presumed first century Near East provenance or a totally unique image-making process.

Then came the carbon-dating fiasco of 1988. It is important first to note that the world's carbon-dating experts met in 1985 for the Congress of Trondheim, Norway, and in 1986 in Turin, as a result of which they set forth a detailed Protocol they recommended be followed for any carbon-dating of the Shroud cloth. Rarely has such a protocol been so pointedly ignored:

(1) It proposed the utilization of seven laboratories; four using the Libby technique with 45 years of experience, and three using the new AMS, or accelerator technique, with less than five years of experience. Only the latter three were used.

(2) It proposed that samples be taken from three to five locations on the Shroud. A sample was taken from only one location, at an extreme corner of the cloth which shows almost black on all photographs because it is the place where the Shroud was hand-held in earlier times and by sweaty, grimy hands; also, it is a suspect area that may have been darned in 1532, and may involve a strip not original to the Shroud, as well as being near a burned area.
(3) It proposed that a scientist-observer be present at sample-taking, but none was.
(4) It proposed that the sample-taking and control-cloth arrangement be "double-blind." Instead, representatives of each of the laboratories (Zurich, Oxford, and Tucson) were present, and when ancient pieces of control-cloth were handed over, they were labeled with location and age.

It is not profitable to speculate on the propriety of the conduct of any persons involved, but subsequent news reports make clear that industry politics have given these and other AMS laboratories and personnel advantages they did not have before.

What is most important in this aftermath, however, is a factor some archaeologists (who are the end-users of carbon-dating services) warned of a number of years previously—namely, that carbon-dating of the Shroud cloth may not be technically possible with present-day laboratory techniques and practices. Moreover, archaeologists say that, when dating an artifact, if two or more date-estimates are at variance, the carbon-date is the one thrown out as being the least reliable.

First, I will mention two of the less-provable obstacles in carbon-dating the Shroud cloth: In the 1970s, two researchers separately suggested that the 1532 fire at Chambery, France, which caused the silver reliquary to drip molten silver onto the cloth, also may have created a "pressure-cooker effect" of driving known contaminants on the cloth *into* the molecules of the cloth, so that the carbon content is skewed. More recently, at the Rome Symposium of 1993 and subsequently, Dmitri Kouznetsov of the Sedov Laboratory in Moscow has asserted that during the 1532 fire the molten silver acted as catalyst for carboxylation of the cellulose, so that subsequently the cloth becomes enriched with carbon, making the cloth younger.

However, much more certain is the work of Leoncio Garza-Valdes and associates at the University of Texas in San Antonio, which he reported in 1993 at Rome and subsequently at five symposia in Canada, the U. S. and in Mexico. Garza reports that a natural microbe, the "isodiametric," which is often found on ancient cloth and is definitely on threads of the Shroud, exudes a gel known as "lichenothelia varnish," which is high in carbon content; the relevance for us is that every century the Shroud of Turin gets *younger* with our present carbon-dating techniques. The laboratories in 1988 did no testing for this microbe and its gel and used no treatment that could eliminate it. Garza is presently working on a technique that will cleanse the Shroud cloth safely and will make carbon-dating accurate. (Shroud samples for Garza's experiments were taken to the University of Texas from Turin by Professor Giovanni Riggi.)

But does that solve everything? Well, hardly.

Unfortunately, a very large percentage of our populations let the news media do their thinking for them. And even more unfortunate is the apparent fact that for the media, "If it's not negative, it's not news!" The result being that when the laboratories reported that 1320 was the median date the Shroud cloth was woven, the media reported it prominently (and gleefully?), and promptly buried the Shroud; there's hardly been a word since from the news media. Even the Shroud Symposium of 1993 in Rome resulted in not even a ripple of news, nor did the six international symposia, 1989–91.

Will anything make a difference to the media? It seems unlikely. However, last Fall the Pope instructed Cardinal Saldarini, the archbishop of Turin, to announce public exhibitions of the Shroud for April 18 to May 31, 1998 (Centennial of the first Shroud photograph), and for April 29 to June 11, 2000 (Anniversary of the birth of Jesus), and in connection with the 1998 Exposition, a Scientific Congress on the Shroud will be held. As these dates get closer, the events might merit a bare mention—we'll see!

For thinking people, there are many scientific anomalies arising from a number of facets of the Shroud mystery which make it a worthy object of interest—for instance:

1. The U.S. scientific group (S.T.U.R.P.—Shroud of Turin Research Project) that examined the Shroud in October 1978 unanimously reports, "Our conclusion that the Image on the cloth is not the result of applied materials, but rather is due to an oxidation of the cellulose that made up the flax—is *still*

valid and correct." This means that the Image of the Man on the Shroud was not painted, and that an unknown event of oxidation *selectively* darkened certain fibrils of the threads so as to make a *superficial* image of a man with accurate details valid when magnified 1000 times.

2. The body image is a photographic negative, but photography was not invented until the 19th century—it is still developing after 150 years. How could a brilliant 14th-century artist have anticipated that technique? And how could he have reversed the lights and darks in order to check the accuracy of his work? And why did he not ever do it again, or admit to his masterpiece?

3. The cloth-to-body distance correlates so precisely that the Image encapsulates three-dimensional data perfectly. A few years ago N.A.S.A. developed the VP-8 Image Analyzer to add a dimension of depth to their stellar photo-maps. When the Shroud image is fed into the VP-8 it produces a bas-relief of the Man of the Shroud—*and with no distortion*! No other image, drawing, painting or photograph has this quality—just star-maps and the Shroud Image; everything else distorts in attempts for 3-D on the VP-8.

4. Scalp punctures and blood rivulets from them, especially as seen on the forehead of the Man of the Shroud, have the characteristics and proper location for both veinous and arterial bloodflow, and yet circulation of human blood was not discovered until 1593.

5. Blood rivulets down the forearms angled and dripped, tracing perfectly the true reaction to gravity for such flows, and yet gravity was not identified until 1666.

6. Most of the pollen on the Shroud (some 70 varieties) came from the Near East and 38 varieties from within fifty miles of Jerusalem and 14 of them grow nowhere else; the Z-twist thread and 3-to-1 herringbone-twill weave were known only in the Near East and Asia until recent centuries; cotton fibers (in the Shroud linen) could have come only by weaving on looms of the Near East. So, why would an artist of Europe go there to buy the cloth since none of his peers would know the difference?
7. Microscopes were invented 1590 to 1610, and yet we find meaningful data in the Shroud image by magnifications up to 1200 times; how could an artist of the 1300s make such details?
8. The feet of the Man of the Shroud have smudges of actual dirt, and it is "travertine argonite," a rare form of calcium which *matches* the spectral properties of this limestone substance found in caves near Jerusalem's Damascus Gate, and no other source is known.
9. One oddity of the Shroud image is that it can be seen only in an optimum viewing distance of six to fifteen feet—closer or farther, and the image fades out of view. So, how did an artist manage—with arm plus brush 6 to 7 feet long?
10. There are some two to four dozen Faces of Jesus made in the early centuries which, by superimposition scientific matching, can be found to duplicate the Shroud Face; so, what were those early artists copying if the Shroud image dates only to the 14th century?
11. Dr. Pierre Barbet wrote (1950 English translation) that coagulation of blood was not understood by doctors in the 14th century, much less by art-

ists. Yet, such is depicted perfectly on the Shroud, as well as blood separation at death (serum-albumin halos).

12. Even the latest Bible versions tell us Jesus was nailed in the "hands." But the Shroud image correctly shows us a medical truth: He was nailed through the "space of Destot" in the wrist, because a nail in the soft flesh of the hand would not support a man's weight. The Greek word "cheir" can be translated as hand, wrist or forearm. This detail was not noted by Shroud scholars until 1598 in Bologna.

13. A spike through the "space of Destot" in the wrist will lacerate the median nerve, causing the thumb to flex sharply into the palm. The Man of the Shroud has no thumbs. Would an artist have known it?

14. The bloodstains on the Shroud are precisely correct, Biblically and anatomically, and are pristine perfect. If the Shroud was *lifted off* the Man, one of two things would have happened: if the blood was still wet the stain on the cloth would smear; if the blood was dry it would have broken the crusted blood that had soaked into the weave. *Neither* happened. The body must have dematerialized in place *without removal* of the Shroud. If the Shroud merely *collapsed,* and was not thrown back, would not John 20:1–10 make better sense in describing the Easter visit of Peter and the "beloved disciple" to the tomb, where Peter "saw the linen cloths lying" and the other "saw and believed"?

15. Although the Shroud had some contact with the Man's body, for the bloodstains are of real blood, the body-image is described by the scientists as "made through space" by an "image-

making process" which they have named "flash photolysis," because the images are *not pressure sensitive,* in that the back and front images of the Man have the same shadow and lack of saturation characteristics—by lying on his back, *that* image should be darker and different if contact was the only factor.

16. Real blood was on the Shroud *first,* because it shielded the cloth; the body image did not "print" wherever there was blood.

17. Rigor mortis details prove death occurred *on* the cross (neck and upper back; right knee cocked; shoulder girdle rigor broken for burial; etc.).

18. The Man was crowned with a *cap* of thorns, not a Greek-style wreath; this would have been correct for the Oriental Judeans, but not for Europe.

19. Pollen grains on the cloth prove it was open to the air in Judea, but those grains are *not* covered by a "colagen binder or pigment" as would be true if the image was painted.

20. This Man suffered a criminal's death but had a wealthy man's burial.

21. The bloodstains are photographically positive (dark on the cloth), *not* negative as is the body image; they accurately reflect events covering some ten hours, from about 5 a.m. to 3 p.m., each recorded pristine perfect on the Shroud.

22. As long as there is *any* image, there must be a residue of paint, stain, ink or dye if it is a man-made image; there is no such residue.

23. The body image is made by the "yellowing" of dehydration, of just the top two or three fibrils of "selected" portions of thread.

24. There is no cementing or bonding or under-

coating to seal the interstices of the cloth's coarse weave, which painters and artists have always used.

25. If this image was made by a natural process, it is one that has never been otherwise recorded.

26. From its earliest years, in legends and in art, there have been claims of miracles and healings through the Shroud. Eusebius and others state that King Abgar V of Edessa was mortally ill and was instantly healed when shown the Face on the cloth. While being carried to Constantinople in 944, it was said that a man possessed of demons was healed when he touched it. Four credible writers report that in 544 when Edessa was threatened with siege by a Persian army, the Image was rushed to the top of the City wall and prominently displayed; the army turned and abandoned the siege. Modern skepticism automatically rejects such early claims, but an event in 1955 is harder to brush aside: In a small village of Gloucestershire, England, eleven-year-old Josephine Wollam was in the hospital dying of a severe bone disease, osteomyelitis in hip and leg, plus lung abscesses. The doctor advised that there was no hope for Josie and she was given last rites of the Church; however, she had learned of the Shroud lectures given by retired RAF Group Captain Leonard Cheshire, and told her mother if she could only see the Shroud she was sure she would walk again. At Josie's urging, her mother wrote Cheshire, and his office sent a photograph of the Shroud Face. Holding the photo seemed to effect a partial remission, and two weeks later she was home though unable to walk. She believed if she could see the Shroud she would be totally healed, and Cheshire was so

informed. He was so impressed with her faith that two months later he took her to Portugal to see former King Umberto II, the Shroud's owner, whose permission was readily given for a rare private session with the Shroud. They then travelled to Turin, where the rolled Shroud was placed across the arms of her wheelchair while she reached a hand into the end of the roll to touch the inner surface. At the 1978 public exhibition, she walked into the Cathedral, again accompanied by Capt. Cheshire, met Fr. Peter Rinaldi, and told him that after healing in Turin, she married, had a daughter, and was gainfully employed.

Almost all skeptics and critics of the Shroud of Turin image claim or assume that it was a medieval painting. At several of the scientific symposia on the Shroud during the past two decades, including the one at Rome in 1993, Isabel H. Piczek of Los Angeles has presented highly impressive papers on this subject. Piczek is a professional monumental-artist with a degree in physics and has won international awards for painting and figurative draftsmanship. She has executed artworks in every ancient and modern technique known, including nearly five hundred giant-size items in public buildings throughout the world. Piczek, in her professional papers respecting the Shroud image, has analyzed every artistic aspect of the image, and has concluded that it *is not and cannot be* a painting of any sort, technique or medium. This conclusion is doubtly important because, she cautions, the Shroud and its image *must not* be conserved *as a painting would be,* "or else we may destroy the only object on earth which is the blueprint of the future of our cosmos."

So, one might ask, "Why, upon the October 13, 1988, announcement of dating, didn't Shroud researchers advise the media of the carbon-dating weaknesses, and of other factors in support of authenticity?" They did!—within 48 hours; detailed statements were provided the media by Rev. Albert Dreisbach, Jr., director of the Atlanta Shroud Center; by Dr. Alan D. Whanger, Duke University; by Prof. William Meacham, Hong Kong University; and by Paul C. Maloney, director of A.S.S.I.S.T. (Assn. Of Scientists & Scholars Int'n'l for the Shroud of Turin). And I have no doubt there were similar statements from researchers in England.

There have always been critics, skeptics and disbelievers. Abgar's second son, Manu V, was one such. The Byzantine Emperor's sons were, also. Bishop Henri de Poitieres of Troyes vacillated by praising the de Charny's exhibition in Lirey and then trying to stop them. His successor, Bishop Pierre D'Arcis, tried to stop later exhibitions there, but the Pope told him to back off or face excommunication. Researchers of this century have found a D'Arcis memo of 1389 (presumably intended for the Pope) stating that Bishop Henri knew a painter who admitted to painting the Shroud image. French scholar Ulysee Chevalier believed it and so did the English Jesuit Herbert Thurston. The late Dr. John A. T. Robinson of England also believed it at first, but he kept on reading and convinced himself that the Shroud and its images were genuine. Just in this decade, Parisian researchers have determined that the so-called

D'Arcis memo was no memo at all, but just a clerk's draft in poor Latin, never dated nor signed nor sent to the Vatican, and with no official copy either in Troyes or in the Vatican. And of course, there has been a spate of sensational books in the last decade that hardly merit comment; one of which claimed the Shroud images were painted by Leonardo da Vinci who, as you know, was born in 1452, after the Shroud had had its lengthy exhibition run in Lirey in 1357.

Although critics' alternative suggestions as to the making of the images have often been made in bad faith, the STURP scientists have meticulously tested every one and found all of them to be seriously wanting. This is an Image that modern artists cannot duplicate and modern scientists cannot explain. Of course, the suggestion remains that this is the Shroud of Jesus and that the Images on it were made without physical explanation and by a spiritual energy as part of a spiritual event we call The Resurrection. This explanation will never be proven, but I personally believe it.

Two papers at the Rome Symposium of 1993 tend to support such belief: Dr. Gilbert R. Lavoie of the Fallon Clinic, Worcester, Massachusetts, demonstrated with slides that the blood and body images on the Shroud cloth are of a man *suspended upright*—as if hanging on a cross, but *not* standing. The body of Jesus hung on the cross from 9 a.m. until 3 p.m., yet he was not placed on his back within the folds of the Shroud until about 5 p.m.; thus, truly a *spiritual* image has resulted in order for the image to show him as if hanging on the cross. Dr. John P. Jackson of the University of Colorado explained that the instantaneous image-making process fits the scientific facts *only* upon postulating that the upper-half of the Shroud (which had been *over* the Man) *was falling through the body-space as the body was dematerializing.* Truly, "*spiritual image-making*"!

Thus, you would seem to have four choices:

1. To believe it is Jesus' Shroud, with Images made by spiritual process at the Resurrection.
2. To believe it is an authentic archaeological artifact with images of an unknown person, and made by some spiritual or supernatural force and control.
3. To believe it is an authentic archaeological artifact with images of an unknown person, involving a single *unique,* but unreported and yet-to-be-discovered creative event that was human-controlled, or a natural process happening spontaneously and never before reported.
4. To believe it is the result of a man-made fake.

CHAPTER EIGHT

✠

A Spiritual Psychotherapist Shares Her Meetings with Jesus

Dr. Loretta Ferrier, who recently opened a professional practice in Las Vegas, is well known for the original techniques that she designed to unite harmoniously the internal masculine and feminine aspects of the total self. As a psychotherapist who emphasizes the spiritual aspects of human exploration, Dr. Ferrier was not at all reluctant to tell us that her first encounter with Jesus occurred when she was only five years old.

"In 1941 we had just moved from Texas to San Francisco," she said in November of 1996. "I was grief stricken because I had to leave behind my precious dog Bear and my greatly beloved aunt and uncle. I cried and cried and thought that I must have done something terrible to have caused this to happen."

Dr. Ferrier remembers that she kept saying over and over, "Why, God? Why? Let me be with my puppy."

Suddenly a radiant light appeared at the foot of her bed. She could see a form in the light, and she knew or felt that it was Jesus.

"Jesus?" she said. "Can it really be you?"

"Yes, my precious child," He answered her. "Weep no more. Dry your tears, for the angels are here with you. You will never be alone. I am always here. Just call my name. You had to come here to this place in order to grow into the woman you must be."

Dr. Ferrier admitted that she didn't really understand everything that Jesus said or what he meant by her growing into "the woman she was meant to be," but she did calm down.

"I never again cried because we had left our loves in Texas and moved to San Francisco," she said. "The next day I told my mom about seeing Jesus and she told me, 'God has something for you to do when you are all grown up.' Then she cried and held me close to her. From that day on, angels began to appear to me on a regular basis; and my mother, who was a channeller and a healer, always encouraged me to trust them and to love them."

Dr. Loretta Ferrier's second sighting of Jesus occurred when she was forty-four and going through a terrible time in her life.

"My fiancé had been murdered," she explained, "and there was great danger around me. I ran briefly to Santa Fe, then returned to the Bay area. Hardly a day passed when I didn't live in fear for my life.

Since the murderer's identity was completely unknown, the next stranger I met could be the same assailant who killed my fiancé, now after me. The assassin could be upon me before I even realized that I was in immediate danger."

Dr. Ferrier remembered vividly that day when she decided to raise the window shades, let the sun shine in, and relax in the tub.

"Since I lived alone, I left the bathroom door open. I was relaxing in soap bubbles when a form appeared."

She looked up immediately, but she didn't feel startled. There stood a molecular form of Jesus—and he was smiling at her.

"Is that you, Lord?" she asked.

"Yes, my child," he answered.

She jumped out of the tub and threw on a robe. "I ran into the living room and fell to His feet. Tears were streaming down my face."

Dr. Ferrier had spent many years studying metaphysics, and she had grown away from her childlike acceptance of Jesus as eternal heavenly lord and had come to consider the reality of the Jesus concept to be more of a religious metaphor.

"I am no metaphor, my child," Jesus told her. "And I have come to tell you that you are safe and that all is well. I am coming, my child. Prepare the way."

With those words of comfort and commission, the image of Jesus vanished and she was once again alone.

"I had been blessed to see my Lord for a second time in my life," Dr. Ferrier said. "I do believe that He is coming—both in the consciousness of humankind and as a living being who will embody all of the characteristics that this world is so desperate for.

"We are now living in the Last Days, and so we will have the severe weather changes, severe hunger and war, and the great sorrow that weighs down the hearts and minds of humankind. No one knows that certain day when He will come, but I know that He will come—and we will reign in peace with Him for one thousand years! In the meantime, those of us who have received such messages and encounters with Jesus must serve to help ease the fears of others."

CHAPTER NINE

✠

Jesus Gave Her Assurance that Her Baby Would Be Well

When her youngest daughter was nine months old, forty-five-year-old Suzanne Falkenhagen of Alabama told us that she and her husband feared they were going to lose her.

"That was back in September of 1978," Suzanne told us. "Little Margaret had cried most of her tiny life, and to quiet her I had to carry her in my arms practically all day long. She was very thin and had grown but little."

One evening Suzanne's husband, Paul, decided to sleep with their two-year-old son Richard in the other bedroom.

"Paul was doing heavy manual labor at that time,

and he needed to get his rest," Suzanne explained. "We had only been married a little over three years, and we had been having some pretty tough times. We hadn't been able to continue to make rent for the nice house that we had been living in before the kids came, and we were just making ends meet in a pretty ramshackle house that needed a lot of repairs. We couldn't afford to have Paul miss any work time, and it was nearly impossible for him to get any sleep at all in our bedroom with poor little Margaret crying most of the night."

At last the baby fell asleep, and Suzanne eased the child down on the bed beside her.

"I was too much on edge to nod off right away, so I picked up the Bible from the nightstand and opened the pages at random to Matthew 11. Soon I was reading verses twenty-eight to thirty that invited all to come to Jesus for their restoration: 'Come unto me, all ye that labor and are heavy laden, and I will give you rest. Take my yoke upon you, and learn of me; for I am meek and lowly in heart: and ye shall find rest unto your souls. For my yoke is easy, and my burden is light.' "

Suzanne felt as though the verses had been written directly to her.

"I sat up in bed and thought for a minute. Although I was weary and heavy laden—and I certainly needed some rest—I realized with shame that even though I professed to be a good Christian, I had not read my Bible nor I had prayed very much at all to Jesus since the baby was born.

"I knew that my recent motherhood should be no excuse, but I had so much trouble with Margaret that it seemed that every waking moment was spent with her. I knew the poor thing was uncomfortable. We had taken her to the doctor several times, and he had given her medications. But Margaret cried practically all day and night."

Suzanne slowly moved away from the baby and buried her face in her pillow.

"I prayed to my Savior to give me some sign that his love was forever and that he was still there to bless me. I thanked him that he had given Margaret life and I begged him to heal her from the sickness that tormented her poor little body. Then I asked forgiveness for having neglected my Bible reading and my daily prayers."

After she had completed her prayer, Suzanne said that she looked up and was startled to behold the image of Jesus sitting on the end of a trunk beside the bed.

"He was dressed in a long, dark robe tied with a fairly thick white cord. His brownish hair was shoulder length, and his brown eyes were warm and filled with love. I also noticed that he wore leather sandals."

Suzanne said that Jesus was "the most soft spoken, loving person" that she had ever met. "I could feel waves of warmth and love moving around me as he quoted several scripture passages to me to prove that I was a member of his flock and that I had been born again because of his great sacrificial act of redemption."

Suzanne told Jesus of her great love for him and for God and for all those who followed his teachings.

"He talked to me for at least ten or twelve minutes, and he convinced me that he loved me and would always be with me.

"Then he stood up and walked to the center of

the bedroom, just below the ceiling which was being repaired and had only the shingles overhead.

"He turned and looked back at me and told me not to worry any more about the baby and about our future. He said that things would steadily get better for us. 'I will be with you and your family forever,' he said."

Suzanne told us that after Jesus had spoken those words, he rose, and she "watched him pass through the shingles as if he were a cloud of smoke."

Within two or three days after the visitation by Jesus, she said, her baby was completely well and had ceased her seemingly endless cries of discomfort.

"All of our family was happy," she concluded. "And whenever any of us ever became glum or saddened by anything, I reminded them of the glorious visitation by Jesus and his wonderful words that he would be with us forever."

CHAPTER TEN

✢

They Prayed to Jesus Until Dad Returned from the Brink of Death

In 1993 we heard about a Colorado family that simply refused to give up on Dad when the medical specialists at the hospital advised them to unplug his feeding tube and permit him to die in peace. Although things looked very grim for fifty-three-year-old Russell Miller after an aneurysm burst in his brain and he went into a coma, his family rejected the doctors' quiet recommendation that they allow him to die.

Miller's daughter, thirty-year-old Kathy Ebert, remembered vividly the shock that the family sustained on that snowy afternoon in early March when their personal physician, Dr. Robert Ibsen, sadly concurred with the specialists at the hospital.

"Dr. Ibsen and Dad had been friends for years, and he had tears in his eyes when he told us that there was little or no hope that Dad would ever come out of the coma," she said. "If he ever did regain consciousness, Doc warned us, it would be on the level of a vegetable—and he would probably never be able to recognize any of us ever again."

Maureen Miller, forty-nine, put her arms around her two children—Kathy and twenty-year-old Randy—and, with her voice quavering and tears brimming in her eyes, she told them that it had to be a family decision. She alone would not be the one to pass judgment on whether their father would live or die.

Randy wiped his eyes on a handkerchief and uttered the words that came to be the family's credo. "We've always been a praying and Bible-reading family that's put its trust in Jesus. I say we keep on praying to our Lord until He cures Dad, and he is home with us and well again."

Kathy nodded her agreement. "We'll make a joyful noise to the Lord around his bed night and day."

"And we'll never stop praying to Jesus!" Randy added.

From that moment on, there was always at least one member of the Miller family beside Russell's hospital bed. Each day Maureen read the Bible with great feeling, just as if her beloved husband were awake and participating in their regular family Bible study.

Randy prayed aloud and placed his hands on his father's head. "Jesus practiced the laying on of hands," he said to his mother, "and I'm simply following His example."

Randy, a sports enthusiast, also assumed the role

of a persistent coach. "Okay, Dad, come on now. I know you can hear me. Come back to us. Come back to us, Dad—right now. I know Jesus and the angels probably want you in heaven, but we're asking them to let you come back to us. We can't give you up!"

Kathy sang all of her father's favorite hymns, over and over again. As often as possible she brought along her ten-year-old twin daughters, Kerry and Karla, and they formed a harmonious family trio. When her husband Marty would join them after work, Kathy's family made a robust quartet that inspired the entire corridor with their joyous hymns and lively gospel songs.

And at least once a day, all the members of the Miller family—including any friends or relatives who had come to visit—would form a circle around Russell's bed and clasp hands in a silent prayer for healing.

Within about ten days, an astounded nurse witnessed the impossible occurring when Russell opened one eye.

Four weeks later, both eyes opened and he looked around his hospital room.

The third week in April, just six weeks after an examination of the burst aneurysm had led experienced doctors to decide that Russell Miller would remain in a coma until death overtook him, he moved most of his fingers and some of his toes.

In mid-June, less than three months after Russell Miller lost consciousness, he was responding to sounds and recognizing members of his family. His mouth moved as he tried to speak to his wife, children, and grandchildren.

In another month, he was able to go home.

"Once Dad came home, he rapidly continued to

improve," Kathy Ebert said. "In just a little while he was able to walk and talk normally. Soon he was joining us in our prayers for his health to be completely restored. He ate meals with the family, watched television, and began to read books, magazines, and newspapers."

By that Christmas, Russell Miller was able to participate fully in the celebration of Christ's birth.

"I know that I have been blessed with the most loving family on Earth," Russell said. "They would not accept the doctors' grim pronouncement that I was doomed to live out my remaining days in a coma. Their unyielding love and their constant prayers activated Jesus' great love and brought me back from the brink of death into a life even more glorious than before."

CHAPTER ELEVEN

✠

After a Miracle Healing, She Could Hear the Voice of Jesus

Our friend Beverly Hale Watson recently repeated the age-old truth that sometimes a person has to be confronted with a major, life-threatening situation before he or she can really understand how powerful the following words of Jesus from Matthew 7:7 can be: *"Ask and it will be given to you; seek and you will find; knock and the door will be opened to you. For everyone who asks receives; he who seeks finds; and to him who knocks, the door will be opened."*

Beverly felt the power of Jesus and his promise at the age of twenty-four when she lay in a hospital bed facing surgery for possible cancer.

"The night before my scheduled operation, my

mind ran rampant as to what my future would hold," she said. "In a split second of clear understanding I realized that God held my life and destiny in His hands. All I could do was ask, seek, and knock—and request that His will be done."

Then, Beverly remembered:

"Instantaneously there appeared at the foot of my bed a brilliant golden-white light, as bright as the sun. Its radiance went from floor to ceiling and was the width of the hospital bed. Suddenly a rush of heat entered through the crown of my head, traveled through my entire body, and exited my feet, leaving behind a feeling of peace and tranquility that has endured for the past thirty-two years."

Amazingly, as Beverly later lay on the operating table, the doctors found nothing.

"That growth, that possible malignancy which had been seen on x-rays, was no longer prevalent," she told us. "I had been healed by the grace of God, whose Son had promised, 'Ask and ye shall receive.'

"Not only had a miracle taken place, but I was blessed with other abilities that did not surface until a few weeks later. One of these was the gift of receiving information from Jesus, who stated that I would bring His messages, along with his Father's, to humankind."

"In your moments of silence, I can be heard," Beverly heard the voice of Jesus tell her. *"For I reside within each and every one of you. I am who I am—Jesus Christ, the Son of God."*

"In my hour of need," she said reverently, "I was shown the power of God. Since that moment, my life has been dedicated to doing His work by sharing with others that which I know to be Truth. Along the way, I have been privileged to share many conversations with the Master Shepherd. He lives! In my silence, He can be heard."

As Beverly listened to that inner voice, words to share for all of humankind began to flow through her, along with numerous visions. It was soon thereafter that her career as a spiritually inspired author began.

"Since my miraculous healing, eleven books have been given through me," Beverly stated. "I am only the vessel for divine messages. However, one of my most exhilarating experiences has been the translation of the Book of Revelation as given by Jesus."

Herewith, as shared by Beverly Hale Watson, is Jesus' message to God's children as set forth in the introduction to the aforementioned Book of Revelation as given by "He who speaks only the Truth":

Distinct Warnings Precede the Second Coming of Jesus

It has been prophesied that prior to the Second Coming of Jesus Christ there shall be distinct warnings brought forth to the people of Earth. As humankind continues to disregard the many advisements concerning the deterioration of their planet, they shall soon realize the severity of the situation. Some individuals will experience great agony at this time, while others will find it a time of great revelation.

Catastrophic happenings shall be prevalent around the world. Famines, floods, earthquakes, and a change in atmospheric conditions will affect all forms of life. Pollution in the air will become more noticeable.

Excessive use of so-called wonder pesticides and herbicides utilized to produce better crops are leaving poisonous residue in the soil. Chemicals detrimental to human health are infiltrating foods and plants grown in these areas. Also of great concern are the severe consequences resulting from dumping hazardous waste products into the ground, rivers, and streams of Earth. These deposits are causing water impurities and death to many species residing in this environment. Little by little, humankind is not only killing itself, but everything else on the planet as well. *Man is his own worst enemy!*

Humans Must Now Pay Heed to the Universal Law of God

For centuries, due to governmental and religious restrictions, the masses have been shielded from a great amount of truth surrounding many life-threatening situations. They have been forced, both politically and spiritually, to accept rules and regulations created by man, rather than by God.

The Universal Law of God states that all people will live in harmony and peace; for if the members of humankind truly love one another, there will be no wars or dissension among them. Nor will so many be exposed daily to life-killing elements—whether they be chemicals, food, drugs, or fighting in combat zones in defense of one's homeland.

Do Not Place Too Much Value in Material Possessions

I, Jesus, look upon the many churches around the world that outwardly appear to be "houses of God."

There are, however, numerous religious representatives eager to make names for themselves by running their ministries like business corporations. They persist with the attitude of the bigger the better. But instead of using the money they collect to assist the sick, the hungry, the unemployed, and so forth, they use the dollars to erect buildings or to invest them for greater gain—which, in reality, provides self-glorification through acquiring assets.

A word to the wise: He who places all his values in material possessions shall find these things have *no* value in heaven!

Churches with Fine Furnishings May be Spiritually Hollow

Some of the church buildings of Earth are magnificent structures, decorated with fine furnishings. One may reason that it is most important to create just the right atmosphere to attract worshippers. It is no secret that people enjoy being surrounded by nice things. However, facilities built for their beauty alone, without concrete religious foundations, are spiritually hollow within!

Did I, Jesus, ever build a physical structure to be used as a gathering place for those wishing to hear my words? Indeed not, for *wherever* ye shall gather in My name, there I too shall be!

It is one thing to have a place to worship. It is quite another to build great structures under the guise of dedication to Me and My Father. Especially when, in reality, these buildings are created to draw attention to the person in charge of that particular ministry. Is this not a matter of the clergy showing success in their occupation? God, my children, recognizes those who are *truly* successful.

One doesn't need impressive buildings to find Me. Each person's body essentially is the Temple of the Lord. I reside within everyone who will open the door and invite Me in, for *I am the truth and the way!* He who truly has faith and trust in Me will experience an inner peace and find love, answers to prayers, and guidance.

Jesus Came to Earth to Bring Total Love and Total Peace

I came to Earth to bring *love,* which was to be shared between all people. For if there was *total love,* all humankind would live in *total peace.*

My father sent Me as His messenger so that you might know of the many blessings that He promises everyone who will commit themselves to Him. I did not come so that man would look upon Me as God. My mission was to bring enlightenment to all who would listen about His omnipotent power, love, and the glorious kingdom that awaits the true believer.

The Time Is Drawing Near to Declare One's Priorities

I, the Son of God, now come to warn all nations of My impending return and to inquire of all, *"What are your priorities?"*

The time is drawing near when all people will have to make a spiritual decision as to where their allegiance lies. Woe be to those who do not take a stand!

Beware of Anti-Christs and the Fallen Angels of Lucifer

It is written that prior to My second coming "Anti-Christs" shall appear. Beware My Children of those who come before you saying, "I am He." Do not be fooled by those who speak convincingly of God's promises and riches on one hand and thoroughly delight in corrupting people both physically and mentally on the other. These false prophets will promise contentment and life eternal to those following their advice, and they will be worshipped by many who stand in awe of their powers.

Remember, representatives under the control of the fallen angel Lucifer do indeed have tremendous abilities. Do not be gullible. Be cautious and listen closely to what they have to say.

Divine Guidance Is Available to All from Their Birth

From the date of your birth, Divine Guidance has been within you. Ask yourself where your thoughts and ideas really come from. When you have intuitions, heartfelt feelings, or premonitions about things, ask yourself what is the true source of their origination. Could it be the Holy Spirit trying to get your attention and pleading with you to *listen* and to *follow* these spiritual directives? Did I not promise you a Counselor when I left you?

Direct Communication with Jesus Is the Most Wonderful Gift

The most wonderful spiritual gift that a person can receive is direct communication with Me, Jesus Christ! When people make this connection, they have all knowledge. With this new found wisdom comes peace within and an absence of fear. Obtaining such a relationship is most important, for it will sustain you in the days ahead.

Anyone who is willing to venture into the unknown and to take up my cross will travel down a very, very, narrow road. They will be met with controversy along the way. However, those who choose to serve My Father have nothing to fear, for they shall always be in His care and under His guidance.

Throughout history, God has sent His messengers to Earth so that humankind might know him. He has never ceased communicating with His children. It is you have stopped communicating with Him.

I, Jesus, came to Earth, as have others before me, so that you might know God. I say to you, "Ask and ye shall receive; have trust and faith that all things are possible; and know that one day, I, the Son of God, shall return!"

CHAPTER TWELVE

Called To Be a Healing Minister When He Was Just Fourteen

Reverend Williard Fuller told us that he was only fourteen years old when Jesus called him to be a healing minister.

"The entire experience was vivid and real and directed straight to the heart of my soul," Reverend Fuller said. "But it was quite a few years later that I had the real encounter that was proof to me of a personal contact with spirit."

In a religious camp meeting, he was instructed by an inner prompting to get up from his seat and to walk a good distance to an isolated place.

"There I waited until a man that I had never seen before came up to me, touched me with his hand,

and broke out in a message to me. I instinctively knew that it was a message from God being delivered to me by the voice of this stranger."

In this encounter, Reverend Fuller was told that he would be used as a funnel through which God would pour blessings on His people.

"This time the awareness of the Holy Spirit stayed with me persistently, and I was eventually forced out of my conservative Baptist ranks because of the new territories that God wished me to pioneer."

About a month later, he was with a small group of people at a nondenominational meeting when he felt a peculiar feeling of joy come over him.

"I raised my arms to praise God and burst out in a heavenly language that I could not stop. I went on in delirious praise. This joy was an evidence to me of spiritual touch."

Fifty-seven hours later, when Reverend Fuller was alone on his knees praying, an audible voice, clear and concise, spoke to him from outside of himself and said: "I have given to you the gift of miracles, the gift of healings, and the discerning spirit. You shall lay hands on people in the name of Jesus, and I shall heal them."

Then, although Reverend Fuller had never believed in visions—and as a Baptist minister had preached against them—he had a profound vision. "I saw right before me the children of Israel traveling to the Promised Land. In that wonderful moment, I was seeing a portion of ancient history."

From that time on, Reverend Fuller was able to manifest healing powers in his work with people.

"I saw cancers just dry up and fall off," he said. "I saw goiters just disappear in front of my eyes. I saw people that had been suffering years from rheumatoid arthritis suddenly drop their crutches and begin to jump and to praise the Lord. I saw people with horrible warts and growths have their disfigurements vanish."

Some time later, Reverend Fuller heard of a healer about whom it was said that he was able to pray for the dental needs of his spiritual flock.

"I traveled one hundred miles to be in a service with this evangelist, and that night he laid hands on my head and broke out into a prophecy about my life. 'Think it not strange, my son, the things that thou hast seen me do this night,' he said."

And then Reverend Fuller realized that it was Jesus speaking through the evangelist. "Jesus said, 'All the things that thou hast seen me do through him this night, I shall do also through thee. And greater things I shall do through thee than thou has seen me do through him!' "

Soon after that evening, Reverend Fuller discovered that the Spirit of God had anointed him with new healing abilities, and he was able to pray for people with dental needs. Within a few short years testimonials were coming into his church that indicated over fifteen hundred people each year had received dental healings and more than twice that number were the recipients of other blessings from God.

"There is no big financial machinery behind my work, nor any monied board of directors," Reverend Fuller told us. "I just endeavor to be of service wherever I am able."

CHAPTER THIRTEEN

✠

Healing in the Name of Jesus

Brother Mandus of Great Britain's World Healing Crusade states in his book, *The Wondrous Way of Life,* that the scores of thousands of men and women who have attended his divine healing services know for a certainty that God answers prayer.

"At such services we pray in the name of Jesus Christ, as He taught us to do, and realize the instantaneous response, because illness and pains disperse, often in a few moments," Brother Mandus writes.

Having Faith in Jesus Heals Both the Body and the Soul

While the sight of people who could hardly walk suddenly moving about with joints freed and pain dispersed is a marvel to behold, Brother Mandus affirms that the healing of the flesh follows the healing of the soul and constitutes a much greater miracle.

> During a service we consciously fix our minds on God. We pray in the name of Jesus Christ and know that in God's presence we become whole—first in soul, then in body. God is the reality that upholds our very existence. At the moment of physical healing we have really entered this inner kingdom of divine love and our Heavenly Father . . .

Brother Mandus states that Jesus, "the supreme authority on prayer," has promised us that through faith and prayer we may remove every "difficulty, disease, discord, or disaster" that may confront us. Jesus, he reminds us, tells us again and again that we are only to have faith and believe that we will receive an answer to our prayers: "And all things, whatsoever you shall ask in prayer, believing, you shall receive."

> Here is no diluted theology, but a living truth that will make all men free. The words of Jesus Christ proclaim the truth that man can commune with God and receive answers to every need. [This] literally means that little man has at his disposal all the resources of the Almighty Father to heal and solve every individual and collective problem on Earth . . . All things are indeed possible, conditioned only by the limits of our belief.

BRINGING HEALING AND PEACE TO THE SOUL

One of the greatest healers of modern times was Olga Worrall, whom we had the pleasure of meeting on numerous occasions before her death in January of 1985. Every Thursday morning for more than three decades, hundreds of sick people filled the Mount Washington Methodist Church in Baltimore to receive spiritual healing from this wonderful woman. And at precisely nine o'clock every night those same supplicants, along with thousands of others across the world seeking absent healing for physical and mental ailments, paused for five minutes to give and receive the healing energy that flowed into them from God through the focus of this gifted spiritual battery.

Olga and her husband Ambrose began their public ministry in the 1930s and established an untarnished record as spiritual healers of astonishing ability. For forty years, until Ambrose's death in 1972, the Worralls worked privately to aid the sick. In countless cases, they found themselves the catalysts for true miracles of healing.

After Ambrose's death, Olga carried on their work alone. She never ceased speaking of her husband as if he were still very much her active partner, and she continued to conduct the weekly healing service at the Mount Washington Methodist Church and to offer both her prayers and her healing energies to all those who came to her for succor.

"In the 1930s when Ambrose and I were giving

serious thought to helping people on a large scale, we decided that we would never take any money for our ministry," Olga once explained to us. "Ambrose decided that he would work during the day for our bread and butter and we would devote our spare time to helping the sick.

The Church Forgot Christianity Was Built on Spiritual Gifts

"When we started our healing ministry, we had a rough row to hoe. The Church took a dim view of what we were doing. Somehow or other, theologians had forgotten that the very foundation of Christianity was built on gifts of the Spirit. Healing was regularly practiced by the early Church.

"So all the odds were against us," she continued. "The Church was unsympathetic with the various gifts of the Holy Spirit, and the medical profession was rather suspicious of us.

"Certain more fundamental Christians were certain that our healing work was of the devil. I always told those folks that we stood in good company, for that is what they told our Lord when He healed."

What was it that Olga and Ambrose supplied the ill as spiritual healers?

"I don't know exactly," Olga admitted. "Perhaps we somehow supplied that unknown extra ingredient that accelerates the normal healing process of the physical body.

"I don't know exactly what spiritual healing is. No one does. Maybe it's somehow akin to electricity. Of course, no one knows exactly what electricity is, either."

People Are Soul Sick If They Have Lost Communion with God

After over forty years of practicing spiritual healing, the Church finally came to respect the selfless work of the Worralls.

"Of course, we never once claimed that we were the ones who performed the healing," Olga stressed. "Only God is able to heal, whether He is working through a medical doctor or a clergyperson or a healing channel. Without God's power, you are utterly helpless.

> Now even doctors are more open to the idea of spiritual healing. I have met many doctors who are very compassionate people. I have even found that many medical people are themselves using spiritual healing. Many dedicated doctors pray for their patients and sense that they may use their medical skills to mend the body—but then there is that something extra that takes over and does the actual healing.
>
> The clergy, too, is now more aware of their responsibilities in the field of healing. I salute the Episcopalians, because they accepted the idea of the need to provide their people with a healing ministry and have healing services in many of their churches.
>
> I am in the Methodist Church. We have been instrumental in keeping the New Life Clinic healing service going because of the healing successes demonstrated.

Our healing services are ecumenical. Christians and non-Christians come together. We conduct a half-hour meditation and prayer time. It is in meditation that we can hear the whisperings of God.

"I feel people are soul sick when they don't have communion with God," Olga said. "Their souls are crying out for this communion, and very often such soul sickness will be reflected in the physical body.

"If you can bring peace into peoples' minds, assure them that they are God's children, that God is concerned about their well-being, that those who have passed on ahead are very much alive and are eagerly awaiting their coming, that we do live after death—then you can heal them and bring peace to their souls."

AN AMAZING EXAMPLE OF ABSENT HEALING THROUGH PRAYER

Some years back an amazing example of absent healing through prayer occurred with the participation of Agnes Sanford, the wife of an Episcopalian minister from Westboro, Massachusetts, and the author of *The Healing Light*.

In this particular case, the patient was the eight-year-old daughter of an Asheville, North Carolina, doctor, who had been hospitalized with a virus inflammation of the brain and spinal cord. The afflicted child was paralyzed from the neck down, and a 106-degree fever raged through her tiny body. She was also beset by continual convulsions, and, despite prolonged sedation, doctors had been unable to control the spasms.

Death seemed only a few hours away until the hospital chaplain telephoned Agnes Sanford.

A Promise to Pray for the Dying Child

After listening to the chaplain's cry for her help, Mrs. Sanford agreed to pray for the child. Then, moments after giving her promise to employ absent healing on behalf of the little patient, she telephoned one of Asheville's most respected physicians, a personal friend, and asked that he be present in the hospital to place his hands on the girl at precisely nine-thirty in the evening. "I'll begin my prayers at that precise moment," she told the doctor.

According to eyewitnesses to the incredible cure through prayer, the doctor entered the child's hospital room where a nurse was using chloroform to try to anesthetize the patient so that further convulsions might be prevented. At that time, convulsions wracked the little girl's body every three or four minutes.

The doctor placed his hands on the child at exactly nine-thirty. He had no sooner touched the patient than a relaxed sigh rose from her lips, and she fell into a deep, natural sleep. The convulsions ceased at that moment, and the girl seemed very relaxed.

The following morning, the little patient was still sleeping. Her right side was no longer paralyzed and, by that afternoon, renewed life had come back into her entire body. Ten days later, she was released from the hospital and returned to her home.

By the following Christmas, the girl was completely cured, and the grateful family enjoyed a blessed holiday. According to all accounts, she grew into a vital, healthy young woman who became the joy of her parents.

A Wondrous Prayerful Relay System

Although this kind of absent healing procedure may seem a strange kind of prayerful relay system to those unfamiliar with the process, consider the words of A. P. Stanley, dean of Westminster, who remarked: "We need not perplex ourselves as to the precise mode in which prayer is answered. It is enough for us to know and feel that it is the most natural, the most powerful, and the most elevated expression of our thoughts and wishes in all great emergencies."

ATTACKING ILLNESS THROUGH RIGHT THINKING, LOVE, AND PRAYER

The late Dr. Cushing Smith of Detroit believed that the cause of all illness lay within our own mental habits, our relationship to others, and, ultimately, our relationship to God. Therefore, he argued, peoples' health should be within their own grasp and illness should be able to be attacked through understanding, proper prayer, and right thinking.

The thing that differentiated his work from that of a psychiatrist, Dr. Smith once remarked, was that he did not confine his investigation to the consciousness or subconsciousness of the individual. He recognized the fact that many diseases originated in the mentalities of others whose negative thoughts might be directed at the patient.

"Operations, drugs, injections only put patients on probation until they completely destroy the errors which threw their bodies out of balance in the first place," Dr. Smith stated in his book, *I Can Heal Myself, and I Will.*

Dr. Smith said that he always began his regimen of healing by attacking fear. Fear, he firmly believed, is an element of every disease that tends to keep the patient in bondage.

To Heal or To Be Healed, One Must Acknowledge God Is Love

"There is no better prescription for overcoming fear than the biblical pronouncement, 'There is no fear in love,' " Dr. Smith often stated.

"Before one can be healed or heal others, he must acknowledge that God is love," Dr. Smith continued. "He must be determined to look for love in everyone that he meets, in spite of the obvious appearance to the contrary. One must approach healing with humility, sincerity, and depth of understanding."

CHAPTER FOURTEEN

✠

Oral Roberts Projects Christ's Love Through the Laying on of Hands

Undoubtedly one of the world's most famous Christian healers is Oral Roberts, the Pentecostal Holiness minister from Tulsa, Oklahoma. Well known because of his regular appearances on hundreds of radio and television programs and the ministry of his worldwide crusades, Reverend Roberts has brought the abiding love of Jesus, the ancient ritual of "laying on of the hands," and the power of prayer to thousands of suffering men and women.

Born a Sickly, Awkward, Weak Child

Oral Roberts was born in Pontotac county, Oklahoma, on January 24, 1918. He was a sickly, awkward child without the strength to pick cotton or to help around his parents' farm. When visitors arrived, little Oral ran to hide, because he stammered and stuttered.

When he was sixteen, Oral was playing in a basketball tournament in Atoka, Oklahoma. Just before the final whistle blew, he collapsed and fell writhing to the floor, blood spurting from his mouth. He was treated, then taken home and immediately placed in bed.

During the next six months, the teenager's weight plunged downward to a feeble 118 pounds.

"Papa," he informed his father, Ellis M. Roberts, a farming preacher, "I've gone the last mile of my way."

Jesus Saves Young Oral and Heals His Legs

Young Oral was unable to use his legs until the Lindsay Saints, a touring group of evangelists from Lindsay, Oklahoma, prayed with him one night until dawn. Afterward, the sick boy said that he felt the Lord Jesus' presence on his legs.

"I am saved," he cried out in joyful realization of his partial healing.

However, he knew that he still had a rough road to travel to complete health, for the doctors had diagnosed his lungs to be afflicted with a tubercular condition.

A short time later, Oral was taken to a gospel tent meeting in a nearby community. The boy sat on a chair padded with pillows and listened to Brother George Moncey preach his sermon.

When the healing part of the meeting began, Brother Moncey placed his hands on Oral's chest and ordered the illness to leave his lungs.

With a sudden bolt of God-energy, the teenager

leaped from his chair. "I am healed! I am well!" he shouted, dashing around the crowded tent.

Later, when the doctors examined him, they confirmed that his lungs were, in fact, healed.

As a marvelous bonus, Oral's embarrassing stuttering condition had been completely cured.

A Miracle Is Wrought

For the next decade, Oral Roberts studied religion at various universities. In 1946, he became minister of the Pentecostal Holiness Church in Toccoa, Georgia, and began to hold spiritual revivals throughout the southeastern states.

One afternoon, Clyde Lawson, an automobile mechanic who was a deacon of Roberts's church, dropped a motor on his foot. Roberts remembers that Lawson was screaming in pain and that blood was gushing from his shoe when he arrived at the scene of the accident.

Roberts knelt to pray for the injured man—and Lawson suddenly stopped screaming.

"The pain has stopped," the deacon said, totally mystified.

Roberts clearly recalled that when Lawson took off his shoe, they found that his foot was perfectly normal.

"I could not deny that a miracle had been wrought," the minister said.

ORAL ROBERTS RECEIVES HIS DIVINE COMMISSION TO BEGIN HIS HEALING MINISTRY

Roberts and his family returned to Oklahoma shortly after the miracle of restoring Clyde Lawson's crushed foot to wholeness. The incident had strangely troubled the young minister, and he experienced a period of spiritual restlessness.

Then came the night when he was lying on the floor, relaxing, and he heard an inner voice command him to get on his feet, go to his car, drive one block ahead, and turn right.

After Roberts had followed these somewhat peculiar instructions, he heard a voice that he believed to be that of Jesus tell him, *"From this moment on you will heal the sick and cast out devils by my power!"*

Taking the divine commission seriously, Reverend Roberts rented a downtown auditorium in Enid, Oklahoma, and held a healing service that was well attended. According to a Roberts aide, there were numerous people healed at the service. One elderly lady who had suffered from a stiffening of the hand for almost forty years had her condition instantly healed.

When enthusiastic men and women hailed Reverend Roberts as a "faith healer," he humbly replied that he merely conducted healing services. "Only God can heal," he reminded them.

Reverend Roberts has remained true to that statement now for many decades. In the early 1950s, he resigned his pastorate in Enid and took over a series of healing services being conducted in Tulsa by Brother Steve Pringle.

In no time, Roberts's appearances were packing the gospel tent on a nightly basis. Hundreds of sick people came from towns throughout the southwest, and Oral Roberts was on his way to honor the word of the Lord Jesus that he was to heal the sick and to cast out devils by His power.

Reverend Roberts has become one of the most

widely traveled religious figures in history, and his healing crusades have journeyed to many continents. A university now bears his name, and the Oral Roberts Evangelistic Association and its healing crusades are being conducted by Reverend Roberts and his son, Richard.

CHAPTER FIFTEEN

Jesus Was His Role Model as Healer and Mystic

There are many wonderful stories about the American healer and mystic Brown Landone, and it seems as though he truly was a remarkable practitioner of the power of prayer to transform and to heal the bodies and souls of his fellow humans.

Healing with the Divine Presence of Jesus

"I will never pray for you, but only with you," he told patients. "Christ said, 'If two agree on Earth as touching anything they desire, it shall be done for them.' "

On another occasion, he said, "God is all—and that means exactly what the word states. God is the essence and the source and substance of all things created by Him. Material means created by God are part of God's manifestation, as certainly as are his spiritual powers."

In 1925, when he was seventy-three years old, Brown Landone was informed by one of the foremost heart specialists in New York City that he had only two or three weeks to live. Despite the warning, Landone healed himself and lived to be ninety-eight years old. When he died on October 10, 1945, in Winter Park, Florida, he had spent a lifetime healing people of every kind of disease known to humankind.

His Crippled Legs Are Miraculously Healed

When he was scarcely three years old, Brown accidentally fell into a piece of running machinery attached to his father's sawmill in the north woods of Minnesota. Because of the accident, he was crippled until he reached the age of seventeen—then he miraculously healed his crushed legs and taught himself to walk again.

"I awakened to the idea of a perfect set of legs," he stated. "I thought constantly of the joys of walking and the healing powers of God. Gradually, I was able to move the injured limbs and, finally, they responded to my commands to walk."

He Receives Degrees in Medicine and in Theology

Brown Landone completed his education with aid from tutors and traveled abroad for several years. It came as no surprise to his family when he graduated from a university with a degree in medicine. When he was a boy and undergoing treatment at numerous hospitals, he had astonished his doctors by writing out prescriptions in Latin for other patients.

Although Brown had always employed Jesus as his role model as the perfect healer, the Landone family was perhaps quite intrigued when Brown later became an ordained minister. And they were undoubtedly quite astonished when he announced that he was departing to study in the holy monasteries in the Himalayan mountains of Tibet.

Brown Landone studied for two years at the Karygupa Monastery of the Red Hats and at the Tungkhara Monastery of the Yellow Hats. It was at these monasteries that he became a practicing mystic.

What did it mean to become a mystic? Dr. Landone's answer to that question was that mystics manifested more of their abilities than other souls.

Always the Practical Mystic

But in addition to his healing powers, Dr. Brown Landone remained ever the practical mystic.

In 1913, he conducted an economic survey of Germany, and he became the director general of the Institute of Arts and Sciences of Paris. He was also appointed by the president of France to act as a special envoy to the United States.

After he returned to his native land, he became editor-in-chief of *The History of Civilization* and acted as a consultant to the Ford Motor Company and the Metropolitan Insurance Company. In addition, he translated many foreign documents for Theodore Roosevelt.

When the fortune that he had accumulated vanished in the stock market crash of 1929, Brown Landone spent little time anguishing over the loss of his material assets. He had enjoyed the transitory pleasures of wealth, but now he would devote the remainder of his life to spiritual matters and to healing.

According to his contemporaries, Dr. Landone was unusual in that in his practice he combined the techniques of modern medicine with the spiritual elements of mysticism. "We should never reject material aids, because everything belongs to the Lord and is put here for a purpose," he stated.

There were times when he worked with as many as fifteen hundred patients in a few months. Those who examined his healing practice announced their assessment that Dr. Brown Landone was able to cure about ninety-five percent of the people who came to him for treatment.

Another of Dr. Landone's incredible healing powers manifested in the unusual success of his absent treatments by mail. His office files were crammed with testimonials from people who had been healed through absent prayer.

Aware of the Date of His Death, Brown Landone Writes His Own Funeral Sermon

When he reached ninety-eight years of age, Dr. Brown Landone began to prepare for his funeral. Although he still had the appearance of a trim, middle-aged man, he drew up plans for a memorial, wrote the sermon for the funeral service, and forecast the exact moment that he would die.

That day, October 10, 1945, he dictated several letters to friends, lay back on a couch, closed his eyes, and passed on.

In spite of his astonishing record as a healer and the wide variety of his activities in many other more material fields, Dr. Brown Landone was never considered strange or eccentric by his contemporaries. As one of his friends commented shortly after his death, "Brown Landone was just a very practical individual with advanced ability. He was America's most practical mystic."

CHAPTER SIXTEEN

✠

A Portrait of Jesus that Heals

We have kept in touch with the accomplished Dr. Ingrid Sherman of Treasure Island, Florida, for nearly thirty years. Widowed in 1995 after fifty-two years of marriage, she affirms that she is "still going strong" in her chosen field of spiritual counseling and healing.

Acclaimed as the "First Lady of Poetry Therapy," she began writing her therapeutic poems and inspirational prayers in 1958, when she was laid up in a hospital with a spinal injury that had paralyzed her whole body. Incredibly, her poetry brought about a miraculous healing that enabled her to walk out of the hospital without having to undergo a spinal operation.

Over five hundred of her poems have been published by newspapers, religious periodicals, health publications, and pet magazines. She has written numerous booklets of poetry devoted to this unique aspect of the healing arts, including *Significant Roses in My Life* and *To Uplift Your Spirits.* Several of her verses have been recorded, some read by well-known motion picture stars.

SAVED BY THE LORD THREE TIMES

In her personal life, Dr. Sherman states that the Lord has saved her three times:

"The first was from Nazi oppression in Germany. The second, the natural healing of my spine. The third, being given the strength to be able to endure the personal tragedy in which an automobile accident took the lives of my sixteen-year-old son, my mother and father, and critically injured my husband."

Ingrid's love and concern for humanity resulted in an oath to God to become one of His servants and messengers and to assist others to overcome daily problems.

The Secret of Poetry Therapy: Words Work Wonders

According to Dr. Sherman, poetry therapy takes three basic forms—reading, writing, and listening. The process becomes valuable to a patient because "words work wonders."

"Poetic words often encourage patients to want to express their emotions orally or in writing," she said. "Thus their deepest emotions are being released.

Once recognized for what they are, the therapist can more easily help the patient."

She has found that traditional poems, short poems with a definite message, and the prayers, psalms, and proverbs of the Bible seem to be among the most helpful poetic expressions.

"Modern verse is often too radical and of a bitter, harsh, or angry nature," Ingrid pointed out, "thus leading to a confusion of the patients' feelings. Poetry with rhyme has musical rhythm. It is soothing to the ear and it touches the human heart and the inner soul beneficially, thus promoting curative powers that heal."

Discovering the Healing Portrait of Jesus

One day around Easter in 1969, while visiting Atlantic City, Dr. Sherman discovered a powerfully wrought portrait of Jesus being displayed in the front window of a bookstore.

"It was hanging from the ceiling by a cord, and as I looked at it closer, I found that Jesus opened and closed his eyes. I was wondering what all this was about, so I went inside to inquire about the painting. Here, the owner of the store told me that people had told him that they had been receiving messages through the portrait."

Ingrid looked again at the picture of Jesus, but this time nothing happened. "Yet I did buy a copy of the painting, which had been done on heavy canvas by a 'Gabriel Mac' in 1874. Once home, I displayed it in my Peace of Mind Studio, and many of my clients asked for copies of it.

"Now mind you, I am of the Jewish faith, brought up in Germany as a conservative Jewess. In this country, I joined a Reformed Temple. So my friends asked me what was a portrait of the Christ doing in my office. I explained that I held him in highest regard, even though I do not consider him my savior."

Ten Years Later, the Portrait Returns to Heal and Inspire

In 1975, Ingrid and her husband moved to Florida, where she opened another studio by converting the carport in the back of the house.

"I had dismantled the portrait of Jesus before we moved, and it was not until 1985, ten years later, that I reassembled it and displayed it in a spot where everyone could see it.

"I began to refer to Jesus as my spiritual brother, and I found that, little by little, I began receiving messages through the portrait. Since I am a healer, I would talk to him about my clients, and he helped me in numerous cases.

"He also revealed answers to my clients' questions by writing words in bold letters across his forehead or by fashioning illustrative visions. Each one of my clients was given an appropriate explanation, which in every instance turned out to be the plain truth."

The following are a number of examples, which Dr. Sherman provided from her files:

- On January 1, 1992, Mrs. M. N. gazed at the portrait and perceived an image of her angelic guide in a long gown.
- On March 22, 1992, Mr. E. O. looked at Jesus' image and saw a vision of a government officer raising his hand, a scene that assured the gentle-

man that he would be sworn in as an American citizen.

- Mrs. D. H. looked at the portrait on April 13, 1992 and clearly saw the word "WHOLE" manifest on Jesus' forehead, indicating that she would soon be well.
- On January 1, 1993, Ingrid herself beseeched the portrait for a healing of her tooth and Jesus granted the healing.
- Mr. K. K. sighted the angel Gabriel on Jesus' forehead on October 4, 1993 and was healed of his spinal trouble.
- On April 24, 1995, Mr. H. A. received a vision of his spiritual guide.
- Mr. D. C. saw the image of his late father dressed as a clown appear on the portrait on August 13, 1996 and was pleased with the sign, as his father had always been a great joker.

The Portrait Sheds Tears for a Disbeliever

As time has gone on, Ingrid said that she has grown fonder and fonder of Jesus.

"I call him 'Joshua,' his Hebrew name," she said. "He responds to this name, and I have received some very high spiritual guidances through him. In fact, he has helped me with many instantaneous healings, and I have every hope that he will help me with others in the future."

Ingrid said that recently, when they were discussing the Christ in one of her metaphysical classes, a Christian lady declared that she no longer believed in Jesus.

"At that very moment, the portrait suddenly shifted, and my students could clearly see the Christ shedding a few tears. The lady felt very embarrassed. She apologized to Jesus and asked forgiveness."

Dr. Ingrid Sherman told us that lately she has been asking Jesus to grant her the power to heal AIDS and Alzheimer's disease.

"Apparently he has heard my plea, for he has dictated a short testimony for people who suffer from these diseases to fill out in order to receive a healing."

Will Jesus Return in 2001?

In her opinion, "Jesus of Nazareth was the most scientific man who ever trod the globe. He was more spiritual than all other earthly personalities."

She stated that she is also confident that some time soon the Christ will return to Earth.

"I place it in the year 2001. He will bring with him a better world for everyone to live in. It will be a world without disease or sin or even death. It will be solely an existence of love, laughter, joy, and happiness."

CHAPTER SEVENTEEN

✠

Their Prayers to Jesus Conquered a Demon

How you interpret the following story will depend on your own spiritual and intellectual biases. Some will be content to believe that Peggy and Dolores used the focus of their prayer power to heal a friend of mental confusion and that the "demon" in question was only symbolic of the disease of paranoid schizophrenia. Others will remember the biblical warning that we must face powers and principalities from both the seen and unseen worlds.

In the winter of 1989, twenty-year-old Peggy Ludvigsen happily accepted an invitation to spend a portion of her college vacation time with her older sister, Dolores Alstad, in St. Louis, Missouri. Dolores's husband, Martin, was on an extended business trip to the Middle East and would be gone for over a month. Peggy would provide her sister with both comfort and companionship during the lonely weeks ahead.

The two sisters were pleased to share one another's company once more, as they had always been quite close, though Dolores was five years older. They began going out to movies and fine restaurants and on a number of occasions met socially with certain of Dolores's and Martin's friends. Dolores teased her kid sister that she would even have her fixed up with a beau before she returned to college.

One of Dolores's friends was Sylvia Vanhouten, an elderly woman who had an apartment across the hall from her in the apartment building where she had lived before she married Martin. Mrs. Vanhouten was a remarkable woman, full of tales from the past and generous with her wry opinions of the present and the future. Peggy had been fascinated by the woman, and one night as the two sisters sat up late talking, she inquired about her health.

"As a matter of fact," Dolores said, becoming very serious, "I have heard through mutual friends that she hasn't been well lately. I've been meaning to call on her."

"We must do so," Peggy urged. "She's such a dear woman. I always used to love talking with her when I would come to visit you in your old apartment. Let's stop by and see her tomorrow."

Just as they were arriving for their visit, a tall, balding man, who had just exited Mrs. Vanhouten's apartment, stopped them. "Are you ladies planning to see Mrs. Vanhouten?" he inquired.

Peggy and Dolores were puzzled by the man's direct question, but they answered that they were friends of Sylvia Vanhouten.

The man reached into his pocket and handed them a card. "I'm Dr. Schildkraut. I'm very sorry, but I must ask that you not visit her."

The doctor then quietly explained that Mrs. Vanhouten was suffering from a mental disorder known as paranoid schizophrenia. Although she had periods of lucidity, her mind had been slipping for quite some time.

"Perhaps if we only stayed for a few minutes," Peggy persisted. "She's really been a dear friend of my sister's for several years."

Dr. Schildkraut shook his head, and his manner became quite stern. "Your friend is obsessed with the bizarre idea that her body has been invaded by a demon."

"Mrs. Vanhouten?" Dolores frowned her disbelief. "She's too tough minded to give in to such thoughts. The only thing she's ever been obsessed with is women's-rights issues."

Dr. Schildkraut pursed his lips before he replied. "She may have been tough minded when you knew her, but now she persists in believing that some denizen of Hell is trying to possess her mind. The effects of her delusion are steadily taking their toll on her health. I've sent for her daughter to come to St. Louis to see to her care. I'm afraid that Mrs. Vanhouten will soon be too weak to attend to herself."

Dolores and Peggy were quiet and thoughtful throughout the ride home. As they entered the apartment building, Peggy expressed her wish that there was something that they could do for their elderly friend.

Dolores nodded her agreement, then picked up her mail from the box just inside the door. "Peggy," she gasped as she flipped through the various envelopes. "Here's a letter from Mrs. Vanhouten!"

When they entered their apartment, Dolores tore open the envelope and—at Peggy's insistence—read the contents of the letter aloud:

> My dearest Dolores, I am writing this to you while I still can. I don't know where else to turn. Something terrible has been happening to me. I cannot control what I do, and I no longer know who I am. My grip on reality is slipping. My mind feels clouded and confused. I can no longer control my thoughts. Please pray to Jesus for me. I need His grace and mercy.

Dolores looked helplessly at her sister and let the letter slip to the coffee table as she sat down on the sofa. "How awful. Poor Mrs. Vanhouten. What can we do? There must be something we can do for her."

Peggy picked up the letter from the coffee table. "We can pray to Jesus. That's what Mrs. Vanhouten asks us to do!"

The sisters had come from a very religious family. Theirs was not the kind of spirituality that had them sitting at the front pew every Sunday, but their family earnestly believed in the power of prayer and in God's mercies.

But before either Dolores or Peggy could say another word, a very strange thing happened. The letter was no sooner in her hand when Peggy closed her eyes and began to sway on her feet. She managed to reach the sofa before she entered a kind of trancelike state and collapsed.

Puzzled at first by her sister's peculiar behavior, Dolores recalled certain times when they were younger when Peggy had slipped into an altered state of consciousness during prayer or family worship.

She had just begun to relax and reassure herself that all was perfectly normal when Peggy began to speak in a kind of halting monotone. As Dolores listened in astonishment, her sister outlined the steps that they must take to rid Mrs. Vanhouten of the demon.

Peggy said that they were to perform the exorcism in three sessions, three days apart, always at eleven o'clock in the morning. While the two women prayed for protection, Peggy was to hold Mrs. Vanhouten's letter and enter another trancelike state. Angelic presences and the protective power of Jesus' love would hover over them to guard them from evil during the sessions. Dolores was to be ready with paper and pen and take down everything that Peggy said.

"Oh, wow," Peggy exclaimed, shaking her head in wonderment after she had regained consciousness. "I said all that? I just remember feeling sort of dizzy. Do you really think that I was relaying instructions from Jesus or the angels?"

Dolores emphatically assured her that she had said all those words—and with great authority.

"Remember that Jesus' ministry on Earth was greatly concerned with healing and with the casting out of devils," she reminded Peggy. "You said that the angels told you that we were to begin Mrs. Vanhouten's rescue mission two days from now, on Wednesday. Then again on Saturday and Tuesday. Oh, and we're supposed to fast on those mornings, just like Jesus did before he faced his great adversary, Satan, in the desert."

Wednesday morning Dolores and Peggy rose a

bit earlier than usual, excited and apprehensive about their first attempt at helping their friend escape from whatever negative energy had possessed her. Neither woman was certain that they would be successful, and neither had any real idea what would occur. All the same, they had their faith and their determination.

At eleven o'clock in the morning, Peggy lay down on the sofa. Dolores sat nearby, her pen poised over a stenographer's tablet. Peggy began to pray aloud for the love of Jesus and for angelic protection to surround them. Then, with a final reassuring glance at her sister, she picked up Mrs. Vanhouten's letter.

Almost at once, Peggy experienced a weird kind of whirling sensation. Mentally, she asked for the protecting love of Jesus and her guardian angel to be with her.

Peggy felt a sudden jerk in her right hand, the one that clutched Mrs. Vanhouten's letter. She experienced a *knowing* that the envelope was her link to the older woman, and she felt certain that she had established firm contact when she became aware of an electrical kind of energy surge throughout her arm.

And then, as strange as it seemed, Peggy seemed to find herself inside Mrs. Vanhouten's bedroom. She was aware of the elderly woman sitting up in bed, her eyes transfixed in an expression of terror. Thankfully, she was also aware of the power of Jesus and the presence of her guardian angel somewhere near her.

"Enter her thoughts," Peggy heard an inner voice instruct her. *"Learn what frightens her . . . what possesses her."*

Peggy did as the angelic voice commanded. She

visualized herself becoming one with Mrs. Vanhouten, and she was immediately able to hear ugly and obscene whispers.

The voice was threatening, cruel, dripping with malice. "Suffer, woman! No one, nothing can save you. I have you in my power. I own you. You are mine; I will control you; and I want you to suffer!"

Then the hideous voice broke into demented laughter, and Peggy became frightened at its awful malice. She wanted to do something to help poor Mrs. Vanhouten, but the heavenly voice restrained her.

"Be silent. The time is not yet come."

Peggy felt a bubble of nausea in her throat. She began to choke and she lost her grip on the letter. Instantly the connection between herself and Mrs. Vanhouten was broken.

Peggy opened her eyes and explained to Dolores with some agitation what she had seen. Dolores dutifully recorded the bizarre account of soul travel in her notebook.

On Saturday at eleven o'clock in the morning, the two sisters were once again prepared to undertake their mission of mercy. Before Peggy reached for the envelope, they prayed to Jesus for guidance and protection. Peggy was not at all eager to hear again that disgusting and evil voice that tormented their elderly friend.

Just as she felt herself slipping into that strange in-between universe, Peggy heard an angelic voice urging her to have faith in the power of Jesus to cast out evil. *"Remember, we are with you!"*

As before, Peggy found herself in Mrs. Vanhouten's bedroom. Once again, as if she were inside the older woman's mind, she could clearly hear the demon's vile voice. It screeched and cawed, mocked and defied the helpless woman, reminding her of all her shortcomings, her mistakes, her misdeeds.

"But somehow you still resist me!" the demon snarled. "There is still a tiny part of your soul that has not yet totally surrendered to me. I want it now! I want all your soul!"

"Pray the Lord's Prayer! Pray the almighty words that Jesus taught." An angelic voice just over Peggy's shoulder told her to pray and continue to pray with increasingly powerful intensity.

Peggy did as she was told, but the demon pursued its relentless persecution of Mrs. Vanhouten without giving her prayer the slightest notice.

In the next moment, Mrs. Vanhouten was stricken with a terrible seizure. Peggy winced as the woman writhed uncontrollably on her bed. She begged her unseen angelic guardian for the power to intercede, but once again the heavenly being cautioned her to wait and to be silent.

But Mrs. Vanhouten was being driven to the brink of utter despair. "My God, I can bear no more!" she cried. "Release me, you abhorrent thing! Please, Dear God, have mercy! Let me die! Let me die!"

"Repeat the Lord's Prayer, and then say over and over again the line, 'Deliver me from evil'! The measureless power of Jesus will be with you. He will not allow evil to possess you!"

Peggy immediately did as her angelic protector decreed. Then, after a few minutes, the voice told her: *"It is enough. Now you must return to your physical body."*

Peggy said that she wished to stay and ward off the demon.

"It is enough. You must now return. Just one more time, Dear One, and we shall be victorious!"

With those comforting words ringing in her inner ears, Peggy was contented to be transported back to the sofa in Dolores's apartment.

During the next three days, both Peggy and Dolores keenly felt the weight of their serious mission. They prayed and meditated often, strengthening themselves for the task ahead.

On Tuesday morning, they awakened early, as they had on each morning of their sessions. They spent the hours before eleven o'clock in quiet meditation. When the hour approached, they took their customary positions on sofa and chair, and Peggy grasped the letter.

During the two earlier sessions, the demon had been unaware of Peggy's presence in Mrs. Vanhouten's bedroom. On this occasion, however, Peggy felt a sudden surge of power and knew it was her angelic guardian suffusing her with the love of Jesus and the strength to confront the obsessing entity.

"Leave this woman at once in the name of Jesus Christ," she ordered the demon authoritatively. "You no longer have the power to hurt her. Jesus has summoned my sister and me to rescue her, and He has sent his angels to protect us. Jesus is on our side. We cannot fail!"

At the sound of her voice the grotesque entity turned its full attention on Peggy. It came closer and closer to her, uttering foul threats so vile, so hideous, that she became paralyzed with fear. She could not move; she could not speak. The demon shrieked its rage at her, and Peggy felt certain that she would soon be consumed.

"Pray," the angelic voice told her. *"Pray together*

with your sister and with the angels. Jesus' eternally powerful love and protection are with you!"

As if she were hearing the voices coming from faraway inside a cavern, Peggy heard Dolores praying together with a chorus of soft, melodic voices:

"Yea, though I walk through the valley of the shadow of death, I will fear no evil, for Thou art with me. Thy rod and Thy staff, they comfort me . . ."

Peggy felt the paralysis lift from her body, and she felt herself filled with light and strength. The demon appeared to sense her newfound power, and it began to shrink back from her.

"You are powerless over this woman," she told the entity with quiet assurance. "The love of Christ sustains her. Leave her now! Leave now, I command you in the name of Jesus!"

For a moment all was still, then Peggy saw a flash of light and caught a glimpse of the monstrous form vanish into a dark abyss.

Before she was drawn back to her sister's apartment, Peggy heard an angelic voice telling Mrs. Vanhouten:

"Dear One, you were never insane. You were never crazy. You were a victim of a disciple of evil, a demon. You are well now. The eternal power and love of Jesus has driven away the demon that tormented you. Your body and your soul are healed. God loves you!"

Peggy opened her eyes and found herself once again on Dolores's couch. Her body was limp, bathed in sweat. Dolores was sitting beside her, and the two sisters reached for each other. They wept together as Peggy explained how the demon had finally been driven from their friend.

"She . . . she's free, then," Dolores sighed. "She's free of that . . . thing."

"Yes," Peggy said. "But we should never tell anyone what we have done. Not Dr. Schildkraut, not Mrs. Vanhouten's daughter, not even Mrs. Vanhouten—because it wasn't us, you know. An angel sent by Jesus told me what to do every step of the way."

Dolores agreed. Then they hugged each other and cried.

The two sisters decided to wait for Mrs. Vanhouten to contact them before they went to visit her. After all, they reasoned, her system had been under a severe strain, and she would need time to recuperate.

Two weeks later, however, just days before Peggy had to return to college, they encountered Mrs. Vanhouten's daughter at a supermarket. Tactfully, they inquired about the elderly woman's health, adding that they had heard that Mrs. Vanhouten had been very ill.

The daughter nodded solemnly. "Her doctors said that she would not live, but then a very wonderful thing happened. She had been having a terrible convulsion when all at once it ceased. She opened her eyes and smiled beautifully at me. 'It's all over,' she said. And from that moment on, she was better. She's almost ready for visitors. You must come see her. Mother is so fond of both of you."

Dolores said that they would be delighted to see Mrs. Vanhouten again. "My sister and I were very concerned about her. What day was it, may I ask, that she recovered?"

The woman smiled brightly. "Why, it was just two weeks ago. Tuesday, it was. Right about eleven in the morning."

CHAPTER EIGHTEEN

✠

Will Jesus Return in a Spaceship?

If one couples the promises of Jesus' return to construct a new Heaven and a new Earth to be found in Revelation, the final book in the Christian Bible, together with the numerous apostolic warnings that strange signs and sights in the skies will herald the approach of the Last Days, then it is little wonder that many sincere readers of scripture interpret the reports of unidentified flying objects in the skies as chariots that would return Jesus and his angelic host to Earth to accomplish his Second Coming and as mighty vehicles that would transport His Elect beyond the stars to the heavenly kingdom.

When commercial pilot Kenneth Arnold sighted those mysterious unidentified flying objects near Mt. Ranier in June 1947, soon after the end of World War

II, the explosion of the A-bomb, and a series of societal transformations on the home front that many people found disconcerting, it didn't take long for certain sensitive men and women to make contact with the life forms who piloted the "flying saucers." By 1952, such New Age prophets as George Adamski had introduced the designation of "Space Brother" to describe the angels in spacesuits who were transmitting the need for global repentance along with their cosmic messages of peace, love, and intergalactic brotherhood. And, yes, according to many of the Space Brothers, they had indeed come to prepare Earth for the return of Jesus.

Sananda Is Jesus' Name in Outer Space

For the majority of the Space Brothers, however, Jesus was known by his true name of "Sananda." As one enthusiastic UFO contactee explained the "godhead" to us:

> "The Elohim created Earth, like it says in the Bible. The Elohim work directly under the Creator, Sacrana. Sananda—Jesus—is his son, a most high Lord, who came to this world from another to set an example for confused humanity."

We asked about Jesus' death on the cross.

> Yes, well, he was supposed to have lived longer, but the Luciferian element wouldn't allow it. He projected himself out of the body so he would not have to bear the pain of the torture. He appeared dead, but when the soldiers laid him in the tomb and rolled the stone in place, a spacecraft hovering

overhead disintegrated his body and reassembled it in another location. Then, later, the spacecraft picked him up.

When Jesus went up in a cloud during his Ascension, it was really a spacecraft. And the Bible says he is coming back the way he left—and that means he is returning in a spacecraft.

Judgment Day Has Already Begun

In November 1969, a young woman named Robin startled her friends and family when she suddenly became a channel for the Space Brothers. She shook them up even more when she revealed the Space Brothers' message that Judgment Day had begun. However, the fateful process was not to be one terrible day of salvation or damnation, but rather the beginning of the Final Hours, during which humankind was to be given a last opportunity to repair its decadent house before the terminal series of disasters.

> Humankind has strayed so far that many will not be aware of Christ's return. People of Earth! Listen to me! Your Judgment Day has arrived. Give up yourselves to God, for that is your only chance . . . Be alive and feel true life flowing through you. He who believes in God shall not perish.

Robin was prevailed on to ask the Space Brothers where and when Christ would return. Her contact, who referred to Jesus as "Esu," said that His Second Coming would be "where the sun shines in the West and leaves a shadow." She also learned that the Light Beings who accompanied Jesus had never suffered a

Fall from Grace and therefore never required a Savior to atone for them. They were continually puzzled by Esu's interest in humankind.

Pressed for more details regarding Jesus' Second Coming, Robin's Space Brother revealed the following:

> He shall return where his own people shall be gathered. He will not look as you might expect Him to look, but you will know Him by his eyes. You will have seen them before.
>
> Esu shall return around the region known as your Great Lakes. After the great disasters, they will be known as the Western Lakes and will be somewhat tropical in nature.
>
> He will return near water, because water is His symbol.

Church Leaders Speak to UFOs and Jesus' Second Coming

In the mid-1960s, Reverend G. H. Nicholson, rector of the Church of St. Mary the Virgin, Burfield, England, set forth his views that all Christians should be wary of the fearful satanic deception that will seek to delude the entire world in the last days, but he himself suspected that the UFOs were the "chariots of God."

Furthermore, he suspected, the angels within these chariots no doubt had as their present assignment the monitoring of Earth and the preparation of the Judgment Day that will soon be on all of humankind. These "chariots of God" will be responsible for a mass "space lift" of all His true followers and for the caring of these good people on another world while Earth is cleansed in a crucible of fire and destruction.

At about the same time, Father Lambert Dolphin, research physicist at California's Stanford Research Institute, was quoted in the press as declaring: "The mounting evidence leads me to believe that UFOs are extraterrestrial in origin, piloted by intelligent beings. Their appearance in recent years is probably in some way associated with the imminent Second Coming of Jesus Christ."

The Reverend Helmut Wipprecht of the United Church of Christ of Canada ventured his opinion that the biblical descriptions of angels could easily fit "intelligent beings from space." In his opinion, even the Christmas star of Bethlehem was probably a space ship, "because stars do not stand still and hover over one place."

Space Brothers Have Inspired Some of His Best Sermons

Our friend Reverend Milton Nothdurft, a Methodist minister, agrees that it was a starship that led the three wise men to Bethlehem and the birthplace of Jesus. He also believes that the children of Israel were led from Egypt by a UFO and protected by alien craft during their wanderings in the desert.

Reverend Nothdurft saw UFOs for himself over thirty years ago while he was vacationing in New York State, and he is convinced that they were trying to contact him because he is a man of God.

"Over the years, the Space Brothers have given me inspiration for sermons that come to me in the middle of the night," he said. "Later my flock will tell me over and over that these are the best sermons I've ever preached."

In 1936, back in his native Iowa, Reverend Nothdurft was blessed with a manifestation of Jesus. In his book, *Between Two Worlds,* he writes movingly of the experience:

> That night Jesus appeared to me just as plainly as if I had been with him in Palestine after his resurrection. Whether it was a dream or a vision I cannot be sure, but to me *it was real.* He hovered above my bed for some moments, just beyond the foot. He was not standing, but hovering in the air.
>
> Whether he spoke or not, I cannot be sure, but of this I am positive—the peace that I had at that time was a peace I cannot adequately describe. And, unlike many dreams, it is as vivid today as it was in the fall of 1936. Jesus seemed to assure me that all was well, and that he would be with me always. That same peace comes whenever I recall that "appearance."

Reverend Nothdurft is quite confident that while the Dark Forces do most certainly exist, the majority of the UFOnauts are working in complete harmony with the "Father of Lights," the creator, at all times. He is also at peace within himself that his belief in extraterrestrial intelligences and their role in the End Times in no way contradicts anything that he has found in his study of the Bible. In fact, he stresses, his personal sighting of a UFO and his research into the subject "only augments my understanding of many things in the Bible that are vague to many people."

> Jesus said he was going to prepare a place for us who *thoroughly* believe in Him as God's Son. I have seen with my own eyes . . . some of the vehicles by which I hope to be transported from this three-dimensional world to that more perfect dimension where "in the twinkling of an eye" we

shall be "changed," as many people have already experienced and *have come back to tell us about it!*

. . . The Bible clearly defined the "good spirits" and the "bad" and tells us to "test the spirits." *We know which side is going to win, so we do not fear!*

A Prominent UFO Researcher Has a Personal Encounter with Jesus

Dr. R. Leo Sprinkle, professor emeritus of counseling services at the University of Wyoming, is a prominent figure in UFO research who also experienced a personal encounter with Jesus:

As a youth, I was interested both in science and religion. However, as a result of a "religious rebirth" at a summer youth camp, I began to read and explore my religious beliefs. I became skeptical of my training as a Methodist and Protestant and Christian youth.

As a university student, I focused on education, history, psychology, and sociology, with an emphasis on an empirical model of science.

However, my UFO experiences forced me to reconsider my model of science and my model of religion: In 1949, a buddy and I saw a "daylight disc"; in 1956, my wife and I observed a "nocturnal light." Much later, I explored in hypnosis my childhood memories of being onboard a spacecraft.

In 1961, with a doctorate in counseling psychology, I began to study the personality characteristics of UFO experiences, and in 1967 I began to provide hypnosis sessions for persons who described "loss of time" during UFO/ET encounters.

In the 1970s, I was struggling with the possibility that UFO phenomena were both physical and psychical, both material and spiritual, both personal and transpersonal. One night, lying in bed and meditating, I had a daydream or vision:

In my mind's eye, a figure appeared from the right side of my field of vision. The figure was that of Jesus—not only in appearance, but also in "presence." He wore a simple white robe. With piercing eyes, he looked directly at me, commanding my attention. Then he turned and moved to the left of my field of vision, as if he were quietly directing me to follow. Then the vision was gone; however, the effect was profound.

My feeling was so strong that I had received a powerful message—without threats, without promises, but with a sense of purpose: to share with others the ancient message of Love and Light.

The Head of Jesus Appears in the Clouds Over Lake Tahoe

We have known the Reverends Robert and Shirley Short of the Blue Rose Ministry of Cornville, Arizona, for over twenty years, and we respect them as individuals of integrity who are sincere in their beliefs.

In an earlier work, *The Fellowship: Spiritual Contact Between Humans and Outer Space Beings*, we suggest that UFO contactees such as the Shorts, with their emphasis on spiritual teachings being transmitted to Earth by space beings have not only brought God physically to our planet, but they have created a blend of science and religion that seeks to offer a theology more applicable to contemporary humankind. And Jesus maintains a very prominent role in this melding of technology and traditional religious concepts.

In July 1980, Robert and Shirley were scheduled to give a series of lectures in Lake Tahoe, California. Just before they arrived at their destination, their space intelligence contacts informed them that when they arrived at Lake Tahoe there would be some type of demonstration purposely set in motion to show the presence of the space beings.

When the Shorts arrived at a restaurant located at Tahoe Keys, Robert happened to glance at the front page of the *Tahoe Daily Tribune* and was startled to see "the head of the Lord Jesus Christ in the picture of a cloud formation!" Shirley also saw Christ's head clearly depicted in the photograph, and both of them recognized that this sign "was without a doubt what we had been told in advance by our contacts."

Robert and Shirley went immediately to the offices of the *Tahoe Daily Tribune* and brought to the attention of a staff member just what a marvel was appearing in the front page of their newspaper.

"He was also startled to see that a picture that had only been used to report a storm front moving into the Lake Tahoe area revealed the head of Jesus," Robert said. "He went to show several other staff members who were working in their offices. Everyone agreed that the photograph was very unusual."

Later, in his lectures, Robert displayed the photograph and stated that the head of Jesus appeared to be looking directly at the area of Stateline, Nevada, and that this was to be interpreted as both a warning and a blessing to that popular gambling area. He admitted, though, that he was not completely aware of the circumstances that might follow.

"Approximately one month after the appearance of Christ's head in that area, news broadcasts reported that two men, dressed as casino employees, had left what appeared to be an ordinary metal coin cart on the premises of Harvey's Hotel and Casino," Robert said. "Later, they stated their demands that unless the hotel–casino gave them a very large sum of money, they would blow up the bottom of Harvey's with 1,100 pounds of explosives that they had planted in the coin cart.

"Attempts to disarm the bomb were to no avail, and while a robot device was making yet another attempt, it suddenly went off—with the result that the bottom of the hotel as well as the casino ended up in the parking lot. However, with the exception of some broken glass, no damage occurred to any other nearby hotel or casino—nor were there any fatalities or injuries suffered by anyone in the area. This may have been due to the advance warning, as well as blessing, that was given by the appearance of Jesus Christ in the clouds."

Jesus Reveals Time Cycles for New Age of Christ Consciousness

On May 11, 1957, Wayne S. Aho, a former major with U.S. Army Combat Intelligence, saw a UFO land on the Mojave Desert. "The experience changed my life radically," he told us.

But it was on February 14, 1960 that Wayne Aho received what he considers his most dramatic revelatory experience. He awakened shortly before daylight into a state of ecstasy.

"It was as though every atom in my body was reacting to a stimulus which I was to begin to understand as a spiritual experience," he said.

In his quiet, sincere voice, Wayne says that he saw a group of people and heard beautiful, vibrant music. A person who appeared to be Jesus Christ approached the group from the left. He spoke words "to be shared with others which could be the basis of teaching and understanding that would help humankind in the days ahead."

Wayne reached for the pad and pencil that he always keeps beside his bed and wrote down the words of Jesus as they were spoken.

As he understood it, Wayne explained, Jesus spoke of approaching time cycles of seven, nine, twelve, and fourteen years. Since the time of his revelation, these periods of work and preparation brought us first to 1980, which, Aho states, brought us to "the turning into the true New Age of Christ Consciousness or what many have called the Aquarian Age."

During these times, great earth changes and transformations in human consciousness will be evident. "There may be great upheavals and chaotic times as these changes manifest," Wayne said. "Humankind must learn to give up its old ways for the new."

The fourteen-year cycle—1988 to 2002—about which the personage of Jesus spoke was indicated by Him as a time in which many on Earth will come to know other realms of life forms.

"Earth will rejoin her sister planets, overcoming shortcomings which have delayed her unfoldment," Wayne Aho said. "During this time, realization will dawn in the consciousness of all humankind of the magnitude of the true Creation."

CHAPTER NINETEEN

✠

Armageddon Has Already Begun and Time Is Accelerating

Not long ago, we received correspondence from a scientist who holds a Ph.D. in hydrology and works for an environmental consulting firm. As one who is personally aware of the critical nature of the environmental problems on our planet, this man's inner guidance had informed him that Armageddon, the last great battle between Good and Evil, had already begun:

> However, it [Armageddon] is happening in a way which is very different from the way in which many people have expected it to occur . . . It is a battle for men's minds. The teams are now being

drawn between those who choose to demonstrate peace and love for God and those who do not. There will be no sidelines left to contain observers who may want to put off making their final choice until some other time.

The vibrational rate of the planet is being increased. Earth is being raised from a third-dimensional to a fourth-dimensional planet, to a level where it had once been before the Fall referred to by many scriptures. A result of this process is that time is speeding up.

Time is now moving by 20% faster than it was two years ago. This is a gift from God that is helping humanity raise its level of consciousness more rapidly.

In the process of time acceleration, karma, or the law of cause and effect, is also being speeded up. Therefore, people are now seeing—and will see—the effects resulting from their mental thoughts more quickly.

Learning the law of cause and effect is one of the primary lessons that humanity has to achieve. As Earth's vibrational rate rises, only those individuals who raise their personal vibrational rate will be able to survive . . .

Those people who demonstrate war and violence are lowering their vibrational rates—and many of them are killing each other off . . .

Right now, only the more spiritually advanced souls are being given an opportunity to incarnate on Earth. As a result, during the Golden Age, which will be here in a very few years, the Earth will be populated only by those souls who demonstrate peace, love for God, and love for all of Creation.

The Golden Age will arrive regardless of the number of humans who choose for God. The size of Earth's population during the coming Golden Age is up to humanity.

Because of the urgency of the situation, the Christ Consciousness, one of the first two creations of God, is calling for volunteers to join a Love Corps . . .

Additional Commentary on the Acceleration of Time

Back in February 1972, when Brad was one of the featured speakers at the Aquarian Age International Conference in Honolulu, Hawaii, he had occasion to speak with Colonel Arthur J. Burks, U.S. Marine Corps, Retired, one of the grand old men of metaphysics. Interestingly enough, their conversation had to do with an alleged vibrational change on Earth, whereby everything was said to be increasing its vibratory rate to a higher dimension, thus accelerating the flow of time.

"I think a number of people have taken note of this," Colonel Burks said. "In February or March of 1965, I began to hear from people who had the notion that things were moving faster. I came to the conclusion that about February or March of 1965, it was as if each person in the world had started to take a step forward—and he or she stepped across a period of years from 1965 to 1995. Since everybody did it, nobody noticed it.

"After a period of time," Colonel Burks continued, "I found a reading by Edgar Cayce who said in 1912 that there would be a collapse of time, some interference with time, that could cover a period of years near the end of the century. It seemed to me that these words of Cayce offered some sort of confirmation on the giant move ahead.

"It is confusing, because in spirit there is no time, but I've noticed another strange thing. When I made a prediction before 1965, I would be within a couple of days of being right on target. But now I have discovered—and I hear that others have, too—that a prediction will work out all right, but it will be realized faster than predicted. In other words, everything seems to be stepped up."

Jesus Is Calling for Help in Establishing Planetary Peace

Enclosed with the hydrologist's letter was a Love Corps newsletter with a message from Jesus Christ "delivered through a dedicated follower." Although the communication is many hundreds of words in length, we will excerpt only a few brief passages for our purpose in this present book. The message, *I Call You Now!* was distributed by Spiritual Education Endeavors of Santa Clara, California, which granted permission for the words of Jesus to be freely copied and distributed.

> *A personal message to the heart of humanity from Christ Jesus, January 1, 1988:*
>
> If you have ever spoken my name in your thoughts, asked for my help, believed in my biblical reality,

or been grateful for my teachings in any way, this message is for you. And I will speak in simple, everyday language so all may comprehend.

. . . I need your help . . . Until this planet's state of peace is permanently established, I need you—and many like you, to accomplish heaven's present-day plan to save your own physical life, to assure humanity's continuance, and to preserve the existence of planet Earth. Thus do I call you forth to join with me in the greatest enterprise and endeavor we of heaven have ever faced in regard to Earth's spiritual success. Yes, I now entreat you to be with me, to hear my current present-day message . . .

. . . As my words touch your mind and heart, I invite you to proclaim yourself as a true Christian (follower of the God light)—or person of good will—and to align yourself with my life of Christ Jesus as I am in this exact moment . . . Today, please associate me only with my glowing transfiguration into immense radiant light, which is your own promised path, too, if you choose it . . .

. . . I come now to help you avoid the extinction you could create by improper free will choice. Each one of you is a steward, a caretaker. Each is spiritually responsible for preservation of this entire masterpiece on Earth, not just for human life. You are a spiritual custodian of the planet, given dominion to maintain all of God's creation here. Dominion means caring, protecting . . . not freedom to demolish and destroy . . .

. . . [My continuing role for nearly 2,000 years is] to bring you back to a state of individual, and thus planetary, peace . . . You are now called to join me to save the planet from its present emergency. Many of you term me "savior," but I cannot save your physical bodies now unless you cooperate with the millions of us in heaven assisting you, for you were given free will by our Father.

Those who say they are "reborn"—or wish to be—are now required to demonstrate it through actions. Become a truly peaceful person, accept your role as peacebringer and Christ helpmate . . .

. . . You must show that you are that prodigal son or daughter poised for a spiritual commitment to peace. I cannot intervene, coerce, or force you to accept this calling, but I am allowed to set the standards or rules by which heaven will know your choice. And it is this power I exercise now, having been granted that privilege because of the dangerous circumstances of your [planet].

. . . You are a soul, a light or energy field, created from God's nature. That soul is presently residing inside a physical body, or container, on the planet Earth. Each of you is here for the same general purpose—to bring peace. Your particular expression of that purpose will vary one to another but all are important to the final outcome.

This Second Coming of love and nuturance that you personally express will help the planet bloom again with forgiveness, wisdom, and peace . . . Your acceptance of this calling will make the difference. It is your action I need . . .

CHAPTER TWENTY

✠

Christ Consciousness and the New Human

In her book *Acting and Reacting in a Cosmic Way,* Swedish author–mystic Kristina Wennergren advises her readers that they should not wait for the return of Jesus:

> Christ Consciousness has always been within you; it will always be there; and all it wants is to manifest itself through you.
>
> If Jesus is your master and your guide, let him live through you.

We Are Now Entering the Fullness of Time When the Christ Consciousness Will Once Again Manifest

Such spiritual prophets as Rudolf Steiner have foretold that humankind is now entering the "fullness" of time when the Christ principle, cosmic consciousness, can once again become manifest. Sensitive observers of the contemporary scene have taken careful note of the fact that thousands of men and women throughout the world are being activated by a heightened state of awareness that many term "Christ Consciousness." Each of these people is feeling a seed of spirit bringing forth new life within him or her and is becoming increasingly concerned about the spiritual needs of the human souls around him or her.

In Steiner's *Tenth Lecture on the Gospel of St. Luke,* he reflects that just as a plant cannot unfold its blossom immediately after the seed has been sown, so has humankind had to progress from stage to stage until the right knowledge could be brought to maturity at the right time.

Christ Consciousness Transcends Orthodox Christianity

Christ Consciousness is a transformative energy that transcends orthodox Christianity. The Master Jesus became "Christed" and thereby presented us with an example of what it means to achieve a complete activation of the spiritual seed within us.

Consider the words of Rudolf Steiner:

> The rest of humanity must now, in imitation of Christ, gradually develop what was present for thirty-three years on the Earth in the one single personality. It was only the impulse, as it were the seed, that Christ Jesus was able to implant into humanity at that time; and the seed must now unfold and grow . . .

> The being who appeared on Earth as Christ had to take care that His message could be accessible to men immediately after His appearance, in a form that they could understand.

The Awakening of Great Spirit Beings

In Steiner's view, the Christ energy is the catalyst that germinates the seed that great Spirit Beings implanted within their human offspring. There were, of course, the physical seeds of male and female, which intermingled to produce the whole human being. But there was also something in each human that did not arise from the blending of the two physical seeds. There was, so to speak, a "virgin birth," a something ineffable, Steiner says, that somehow flowed into the process of germination from quite a different source:

> Something unites with the seed of the human being that is not derived from father and mother, yet belongs to and is destined for him—something that has poured into his ego and can be enabled through the Christ-principle. That in the human being which unites with the Christ-principle in the course of evolution is "virgin born" and is . . . connected with the momentous transition accomplished at the time of Christ Jesus.

"Greater Works Than These . . ."

"The importance of Jesus was not that he was a human like us," John W. White remarks in the April 2, 1982 issue of *New Attitudes,* "but that we are gods like him—or at least we have the evolutionary potential to be."

White goes on to observe that while Jesus, the man,

was a historical person, the "Christ" is an eternal, transpersonal condition of being. When we distinguish between the eternality of the "Christ Consciousness" and the man Jesus, we can more completely understand the promise given in John 14:12: "Truly, truly, I say to you, he who believes in me will also do the work that I do; and greater works than these will he do . . ."

White envisions Jesus as an evolutionary forerunner of the higher race that will inherit the earth, a "race of people that will embody the Christ Consciousness on a species-wide basis, rather than the sporadic individual basis seen earlier in history when an occasional avatar, such as Buddha or Jesus appeared."

Jesus' knowledge of his true position was what led him to refer to himself most often as "the Son of Man," meaning the offspring of humanity, the "New Adam" who marked the beginning of still higher life forms on Earth.

Homo Noeticus

White gives the name of *Homo Noeticus* (pertaining to higher consciousness) to the evolving form of humanity:

> Their changed psychology is based on expression, not suppression, of feeling. Their motivation is cooperative and loving, not competitive and aggressive. Their sense of logic is multilevel, integrated, simultaneous; it is not linear, sequential, either–or. Their identity is sharing–collective, not isolated–individual. Their psychic abilities are used for benevolent and ethical purposes, not harmful and immoral

ones . . . The search for new ways of living concerns them.

Jesus has shown us the way of the Kingdom of God, White states, but it is up to each individual to take himself or herself there. The promise of Jesus was that all have the *capacity* to grow to godlike stature, to evolve, to rise to a higher state of being.

We are not simply human *beings,* White tells us. We are also human *becomings,* standing between two worlds, two ages:

> Each of us has the latent ability to take conscious control of our evolution and thereby become members of the . . . New Humanity . . . Jesus did not say that the highest state of consciousness was his alone for all time. Rather, he called us to follow him, from his example.
>
> He called us all to share in a new condition, to be one in Christ, to be one in the Christ Consciousness which alone can dispel the darkness of our lives and renew our very being . . . That state of consciousness is what Jesus exhibited and taught—Cosmic Consciousness, the Christ Consciousness, the peace that passeth all understanding, the direct experience of divinity dwelling in us, now and forever, creating us, preserving us, urging us on to ever-higher states of being.

The Master Jesus Came at a Special Time in History

Numerous scholars of comparative religions have noted that in the millennium before the historical

Jesus, a new spiritual enlightenment came to all the civilized peoples of Earth. Its influence was first felt in Asia, but it is best known to those of us in the West because of its high development in Greece and Southern Italy in the sixth and fifth centuries B.C.E. This spiritual cosmology recognized an unseen world of eternal values existing behind the material world apprehended by the senses. Pythagoras embraced this mystical faith, and Plato gave it such a full and rich expression that it passed into the theology of the Christian Church during the Holy Roman Empire's revival of Neoplatonism.

"All major cultures have transcended cultural reality through certain mechanisms known as Judaic, Christian, or Moslem mysticism in the Near East . . . Zen Buddhism and Taoism in Far Eastern cultures," Reza Arasteh, transcultural development psychologist, author of *Final Integration in the Adult Personality*, writes in *Fields Within Fields* [Volume 4, Number 1, 1971]:

> The interesting point is that all these mechanisms have come to us as a "path" rather than as a logic, as experience rather than rationality.
>
> Regardless of language or cultural and temporal differences, all these styles of life have adopted the same goal of experiencing man in his totality, and the reality of all is cosmic reality . . .

Many mystics and seers, quite apart from the Christian tradition, have noted that there appears to have been another great dispensation of cosmic energy that occurred at the time when the Master Jesus was seeking to raise awareness. Some believe that when Jesus preached about a new way that had come from his Father's Kingdom and that had blended with the feminine principle of the Holy Ghost, he was talking about a literal transmission of energy being broadcast to Earth from some higher realm.

Pentecost, some will say, was a powerful demonstration of that energy. The apostles were so glowing with the cosmic energy that they appeared to be on fire to those who witnessed the absorption of the Christ principle into their physical bodies.

It seems obvious to us that such an energy still exists here on Earth. And it appears to be rather easily demonstrable that, in one way or another, humanity has not been the same since the Christ Event.

Perhaps something truly was added to the energy of the planet at that time—call it the Holy Spirit for lack of a more precise term—and hundreds of thousands of men and women are being activated by that same Christ energy today. All over the world, contemporary citizens of Earth are having their individual Pentecosts, as the spirit seed within them is being brought to fruition.

Early Christians Knew They Lived at the End of an Age

"From studying the period in which Jesus and the early Christians lived, it would seem that the people who wrote the Dead Sea Scrolls and other Apocalyptic material, relied very much on their understanding of astrology to help them comprehend what was happening in their period," religious scholar Diane Kennedy Pike once told us. "They had a tremendous awareness that they were at the end of the Age of Aries and the beginning of the Age of Pisces.

"At that time they began to have experiences of the outpouring of the Holy Spirit; and they had the sense that everything was come to a tremendous climax. And, therefore, those who wanted to enter the New Age would have to change their ways of thinking and their ways of living.

"Astrologically speaking," she continued, "we are today in the same kind of transition. We're at the end of the Age of Pisces and the beginning of the Age of Aquarius, and it seems to be that the persons who are privileged to live in such a time of transition—though it is a difficult time in which to live—do have the opportunities that the people had at the time that Jesus lived and at the time that his disciples were preaching of entering a whole new level of spiritual consciousness."

A Time of Transformation

In the 1950s, Albert Einstein advised us that humankind had to develop a new way of thinking if we were to survive as a species. Since that time, many concerned men and women have joined the great genius physicist in suggesting that humankind must develop new ways of thinking in order to discover an inner road to salvation—one that would involve a synthesis of rational understanding combined with the mystical experiencing of unity.

In 1976, Dr. William Tiller, of the department of materials science and engineering at Stanford University, told an audience of scientists and laymen assembled in Boston for a meeting on the "new physics of consciousness" that most of the universe is composed of various, still-hidden psycho-energies, functioning at different levels in different dimensions. At our ordinary five-sense level, Dr. Tiller explained, we are incapable of perceiving ultimate reality. But somewhere, which we feebly identify as the "Source," all levels are one—and time–space–matter are all mutable.

The physicist also asserted that our species appears to be undergoing a biological transformation at the present time that is occurring so widely in the human family as to appear to be mutational.

In the *Life Divine,* Sri Aurobindo says that however the people of spiritual realization live, act, and behave, they live always in the Divine:

> In our present life of Nature, in our externalized surface existence, it is the world that seems to create us; but in the turn to the spiritual life, it is we who must create ourselves and our world. It is this, indeed, that is of our own soul and mind and life and the perfection of the life of the race.

If those who claim prophetic inspiration are correct and a new dispensation of the Christ Consciousness is manifesting among us today, then it may well be that our future on this planet is likely to encompass a total mutation in our biological structure, as well as our consciousness and our social norms. If we are undergoing a metamorphosis into Cosmic Humankind, then we must begin to practice new principles, imagine new visions of reality, and declare new boundaries of human potential.

Prejudices must be exposed as chaotic and destructive. Rituals and traditions must be evaluated to determine whether or not they support or distract the individual while he or she is making an effective transition into Christ Consciousness. Concerned physicists and social scientists have been warning us for decades that we must alter our psyches or the magnification of our foul tempers through technology will destroy our material world.

Jesus Speaks of the Light Within Everyone

Elaine Pagels, writing in *The Gnostic Gospels,* presents us with a translation of the *Gospel of Thomas,* which tells us that Jesus directed all those who would listen to find their own direction to the "light within":

> There is a light within a man of light, and it lights up the whole world. If he does not shine, he is darkness.

The familiar synoptic gospels of our conventional Bibles have as one of Jesus' principal teachings the coming of the Kingdom of God as an actual event to be expected in history. In the *Gospel of Thomas,* Jesus ridicules those who think of the Kingdom of God in literal terms, as if it were a specific place.

> The Kingdom is inside of you, and it is outside of you. When you come to know yourselves, then . . . you will realize that you are the sons of the living Father.

When will the Kingdom of God come?

> He said to them, "What you look forward to has already come, but you do not recognize it."

It seems apparent that Jesus considered the Kingdom of God to represent a state of transformed consciousness:

> "Shall we, then, as children enter the Kingdom?" Jesus said to them, "When you make the two one and when you make the inside like the outside and the outside like the inside and the above like the below and when you make the male and the female one and the same . . . you enter the [Kingdom].

For many sincere and devout seekers of Christ Consciousness, their earnest prayer might well be that as they open the door to the future, they may discover that they are also opening the door to the true Kingdom of God.

If Jesus Came Today, Would He Be Christian?

The late Alan Watts often expressed despair over those who practiced "the pestiferous arrogance of 'white' Christianity—with all the cruel self-righteousness of its missionary zeal." Today, he argued, when we are being exposed to "all the riches of Earth's varying cultures and religions," there is no excuse for "parochial fanaticism."

In *Earth* magazine, November 1971, he wrote that Christianity would seem ever so much more valid if it would stop insisting on being an oddity:

> Christianity has universality . . . only in recognizing that Jesus is one particular instance and expression of a wisdom which was also, if differently, realized in the Buddha, [and] Lao-tzu . . .
>
> This wisdom is that none of us are brief island existences but forms and expressions of one and the same eternal "I am" waving in different ways,

> such that, whenever this is realized to be the case, we wave more harmoniously with other waves.

Some years ago, Brad corresponded with the marvelous Sir Alister Hardy, D.Sc., F.R.S., an emeritus professor at Oxford University, a marine biologist, and an ecologist who, in his later years, established the Religious Experience Research Unit at Manchester College. In the chapter "Would Jesus Christ Be Christian?" in his provocative book, *The Divine Flame,* Sir Alister doubts whether Jesus would have preached of a God who would be appeased by the cruel sacrifice of a tortured body.

"Surely," he mused, "the parable of the prodigal son must belong to quite a different religion."

> What a paradox it is. To me Jesus speaks of reality—the most brilliant burning of the divine flame in all history . . . Yet I find so much in orthodox Christianity that repels me . . . I cannot accept . . . the hypothesis that the appalling death of Jesus was a sacrifice in the eyes of God for the sin of the world, or that God, in the shape of his son, tortured himself for our redemption . . . I find such religious ideas to be amongst the least attractive in the whole of anthropology. To me they belong to quite a different philosophy . . . from that of the religion that Jesus taught.

Seth Speaks of the Return of Christ and His New Religion

"Seth," the multidimensional being that was channeled by the late Jane Roberts, had some fairly specific predictions about Christ, his return, and the new

Christianity of the future. In *Seth Speaks: The Eternal Validity of the Soul,* the spirit being spoke of the continuing drama of Jesus Christ:

> [The Christ] drama continues to exist. It does not belong . . . to your past. Only you have placed it there . . . and the spirit of Christ, in your terms, is legitimate.
>
> Whether or not the crucifixion occurred physically, it was a psychic event, and exists—as do all the other events connected with the drama . . . The psychic event affected your world quite as much as the physical one, as is obvious. The whole drama occurred as a result of mankind's need . . .
>
> Christ will not come at the end of your world . . . He will not come to reward the righteous and send evildoers to their doom. He will, however, begin a new religious drama . . . As happened once before . . . he will not be generally known for who he is . . .
>
> He will return to straighten out Christianity . . . By that time, all religions will be in severe crisis . . . His message will be that of the individual in relation to All That Is. He will clearly state methods by which each individual can attain a state of intimate contact with his own entity . . . By 2075, all of this will be already accomplished.
>
> . . . As this metamorphosis takes place, it will initiate a metamorphosis on a human level . . . as man's inner abilities are accepted and developed . . . Human personality will reap benefits that now would seem unbelievable . . .

CHAPTER TWENTY-ONE

✠

An Attorney in Washington, D.C., Receives the New Gospels of Jesus

Dr. John Paul Gibson had always been confused by certain religious matters until a most remarkable thing happened to him in New York in 1945.

A total stranger in a restaurant began a discussion with him about the spiritual gifts of God and mentioned the fact that new revelations had come to his attention in a book entitled *Messages from Jesus and Celestials* that had been received through the gift of automatic writing of a James E. Padgett in Washington, D.C. And then, to Dr. Gibson's delight, his new friend presented him with a copy of the book.

Upon a close examination of the inspired volume, Dr. Gibson found that his personal search for the "Truths of the Father," that, in his evaluation, fulfilled the Second Coming of Jesus on Earth, had been realized in the words received by James Padgett. For the next three years, he studied Volumes I and II of Padgett's transcriptions, and he based sixty sermons on their texts. During the same time, he corresponded with Dr. Leslie R. Stone, the editor of the books, who suggested minor revisions in the sermons, then granted permission for Dr. Gibson to use them as he saw fit.

"Dr. Leslie R. Stone was a close friend of James Padgett, and he was present when he was receiving communication from the various spirit writers," Dr. Gibson explained to Brad Steiger in correspondence some years ago.

"Some evenings Padgett received as many as forty pages of material through the gift of automatic writing. Jesus and the other celestial writers were able to write through him after he had received Divine Love in sufficient quantity."

A Conservative Lawyer Began to Receive Messages from Jesus

Padgett was a practical-minded lawyer with thirty-five years of experience when, some time in 1914, he began to receive messages from the spirit world that dealt primarily with subjects of a spiritual and religious nature. Padgett had been reared in an orthodox Protestant church, and until the automatic writing began, had remained steadfastly conservative in his beliefs.

For a long time, Padgett resisted the notion that a

number of these communications were coming from Jesus. But, as he wrote in a letter to a Protestant minister on December 28, 1915, "the evidence of the truth of the origin of these messages became so convincing, not only from the great number and positiveness of the witnesses, but from the inherent and unusual merits of the contents of the messages, that I was forced to believe. And now I say to you that I believe in the truth of these communications with as little doubt as I ever believed in the truth of a fact established by the most positive evidence in court.

"I wish further to say that to my own consciousness I did no thinking in writing the messages. I did not know what was to be written at the time except the word that the pencil was writing."

His Brain and Hand Were Controlled to Convey the Exact Words

According to Dr. Leslie R. Stone: "Mr. Padgett told me that when his brain and hand were controlled by the spirit while receiving the writings, he did not know in advance what the next words or sentences were to be written.

"If he, when receiving the writings . . . allowed his own mind to become active at the time . . . the spirit communicating would stop controlling his brain until he had regained the inactive state so that the spirit could convey through his brain the exact words it desired to write."

Divine Love Altered the Quality of His Brain

Dr. Gibson explained that Padgett had been told by celestial spirits that he must pray to the heavenly

Father for divine love with all the earnest, sincere longings of his soul.

"When this Love came into his soul in sufficient abundance, it changed the quality of his brain into that high quality that enabled the spirits to write through him the highest truths that had been lost to the world after the earliest followers of Jesus died—and which truths they were so anxious to put into print so that they might be given out to the world."

Dr. Gibson Establishes a Foundation to Protect the Writings

After many visits to Washington, D.C., and a ten-year association with Dr. Stone, Dr. Gibson became concerned about the safety of the many writings left by James Padgett. At that time, less than half of the material had been transcribed or printed, and Dr. Stone was getting along in years. Dr. Gibson began earnestly to suggest that some kind of foundation be established to preserve this new gospel of Jesus.

In the fall of 1955, Dr. Stone informed him that Jesus had selected a second instrument who was qualified to continue the work where Padgett had left off. On November 7, 1955, in his hotel room in Washington, D.C., Dr. Gibson witnessed the first message from Jesus through the new receiver (who has chosen to remain anonymous). The communication affirmed Dr. Gibson "among the disciples who are working to spread the Word of God" and offered the other members of their group encouragement for the establishment of a foundation that would preserve the new revelations.

Several meetings with attorneys in the next two months produced the resolution of the final details that would permit the incorporation on January 12, 1956, of the Dr. Leslie Stone Foundation, so named to honor him for his thirty-year service on behalf of the Padgett writings. On January 2, 1958, the Foundation Church of the New Birth was established, replacing the Stone Foundation, which had been found to be unworkable for a successful church operation with a tax-exempt status.

The Bylaws Are Approved by Jesus, Master of Celestial Heavens

Dr. Gibson said that at the first meeting of the new church, bylaws that were two years in preparation were submitted by the secretary and approved by their leader, Jesus of Nazareth, Master of the Celestial Heavens.

"At the close of each meeting thereafter, we waited for comments and instructions from our Leader regarding the business at hand, either approving or disapproving the items."

Here, with the permission of Dr. Gibson, are a number of excerpted revelations from the *True Gospel Revealed Anew* by Jesus (originally published by Church of the New Birth, Washington, D.C.):

The Real Truth of Life on Earth and What It Means to Mortals

. . . There is in all men the potentiality of becoming a part of the Divine Essence. But in order for them to partake of this Divinity they must let the Love of the Father in its highest nature, enter into their souls and make them at-one with Him . . . In order for men to receive this higher Love, they must do the will of the Father while on Earth . . .

The earth is the great plane of probation, and the development of the souls of men depends upon their correct living in accordance with those principles in which the Father has established as the means whereby they may receive this condition of Love, which alone can make them at-one with Him.

No man can of himself become fulfilled with this love, for in only one way will it come into his soul; and this is by prayer to the Father for its inflowing . . . When people realize the truth that prayer ascends to the Father and is heard by Him and answered, they will understand the great mission and benefit of prayer.

. . . Let not people be content with trying to live good moral lives. They must seek with all their hearts the Love that makes them truly angels of God; and such angels, as by reason of the Divinity which such love brings them, can feel and realize the certainty that they are immortal. Immortality is only of God; and anything less than God or His Divine Essence, which makes the creature a part of the Divinity, is not immortal.

. . . Life on Earth is an important part of the great eternity of living, and people should realize this to the fullest meaning and not think the planet is a mere stopping place where the spirit is enfolded in flesh only for the pleasures and gratification of its carnal appetites. This Earth life is like a fleeting shadow of the spirit life, but it is important to the happiness which people may enjoy in the future. It is the most important period of a person's whole existence—and the way that such life is lived may determine the whole future of the person . . . Let all seek this Divine Love, and in faith they will find it and forever be one with the immortal Father . . .

Jesus and Humankind's Gift of Immortality

. . . When the gift [the possibility of becoming immortal] was bestowed upon humans, it was also bestowed upon all those who were then living in the spirit world, but they could obtain only in the way that was provided for man to obtain it. Understand me, everything that was lost by Adam's fall was restored by my coming with the restored gift; and it embraced every spirit who had ever lived as mortal and every mortal who thereafter lived up to the present time.

. . . When, after my death, [the Bible says] I descended into hell . . . the true meaning is that I went into the world of spirits. I proclaimed to the spirits the truth of the bestowal of this restored life which had been lost by Adam's disobedience.

. . . In the future . . . all . . . spirits or mortals, will possess that soul quality or potentiality until the great day of judgment . . . When that day comes, those who are without this divine essence in their souls will be forever deprived of the privilege of receiving this Great Gift . . . And after that time, those spirits who have never acquired this divine nature will be permitted to live merely as spirits enjoying their natural love. This is the second death. Adam's was the first. The great day of judgment will declare the second. And after that, never again will man have the opportunity of partaking of this divine Essence of the Father and "becoming as one of the gods."

. . . The opportunity is now given and will in the future be given to all humans and spirits who become the children of the Father in the angelic and divine sense . . .

. . . Ultimately . . . sin and error will be destroyed entirely . . . So you see, immortality does not pertain to the physical body or to the spiritual body or to the soul unqualifiedly, but to those qualities of the soul which make it possible for the soul to become in its nature divine.

And immortality does not mean mere continuous existence, because every soul and every spirit may live through all eternity in their individualized form. When it was said in the Bible that I brought immortality and life to light, it did not mean that I showed men merely that they would, as spirits, continue to live forever; but it meant that they would live forever in the Father's Kingdom with natures Divine . . .

A Prayer from Jesus

Our Father, who art in Heaven, we recognize that Thou art Holy and loving and merciful and that we are Thy Children—not the subservient, sinful, and depraved creatures that our false teachers would have us believe. We are the greatest of Thy creation, the most wonderful of all Thy handiworks, and the objects of Thy great soul's love and tenderest care.

Thy will is that we become at-one with Thee and partake of Thy great love which Thou has bestowed upon us through Thy mercy . . .

We pray that Thou wilt open up our souls to the inflowing of Thy love [and when our souls are open] then may come Thy Holy Spirit to bring into our souls this, Thy love, in great abundance until our souls shall be transformed into the very essence of Thyself; and that then may come to us faith—such faith as will cause us to realize that we are truly Thy children and one with Thee in very substance and not in image only.

Let us have such faith as will cause us to know that Thou art our Father and the bestower of every good and perfect gift, and that only we, ourselves, can prevent Thy love changing us from the mortal into the immortal.

Let us never cease to realize that Thy Love is waiting for all of us and that when we come to Thee, in faith and earnest aspiration, Thy love will never be withheld from us.

Keep us in the shadow of Thy love every hour and moment of our lives and help us to overcome all temptations of the flesh and the influence of the powers of the evil ones, which so constantly surround us and endeavor to turn our thoughts away from Thee to the pleasures and allurements of the world.

We thank Thee for Thy love and the privilege of receiving it, and we believe that Thou art our Father—the loving Father who smiles upon us in our weakness and is always ready to help us and take us to His arms of love.

We pray thus with all the earnestness and sincere longings of our souls, and trusting in Thy love, give Thee all the glory and honor and love that our finite souls can give.

CHAPTER TWENTY-TWO

✠

The Christ Spirit Speaks from a New Hampshire Mountaintop

In the summer of 1969, in the company of his friend Professor Charles H. Hapgood, Brad Steiger drove his Chevrolet station wagon to what seemed to be the very top of a New Hampshire mountain. The primitive road that the men followed was nothing more than two deep ruts in hard-packed dirt, punctuated here and there with large rocks. One of those solid mineral punctuation marks punctured the wagon's oil pan on the way back down.

The object of their quest was a mountaintop mystic named Elwood Babbitt whom Hapgood, a professor at Keene State College, had been studying for over three years. According to Hapgood, dozens of spirit personalities had been manifesting through Babbitt's mediumship, and during the course of his conversations with many of the disembodied entities, he had discovered what he believed to be countless proofs of authenticity. The professor contended that throughout his dialogues with more than one hundred spirits, each of the ethereal personalities had remained distinct and self-consistent, no matter how many times he interrogated them.

In Hapgood's considered opinion, no human mind could possibly have produced such a vast spread of varied information from so many different narrators. He wished Brad to visit Babbitt in his company and confirm the medium's extraordinary abilities.

Although Brad did engage in a number of interesting conversations with a number of spirit entities that day and was favorably impressed with Elwood Babbitt's mediumship, he was quite suprised when, in 1981, Professor Hapgood sent him a copy of his book *Talks with Christ and His Teachers Through the Psychic Gift of Elwood Babbitt.*

When he had sat with Hapgood and Babbitt in the medium's mountain home twelve years before, Brad had been told that if he wished he might contact the spirits of such luminaries as Abraham Lincoln, Sam Clemens, and Sigmund Freud—but he did not recall being informed that communication with Jesus was an option.

In his introduction to the book that he coauthored with Babbitt, Professor Hapgood makes it clear that he had not actually spoken with the divine person of Jesus Christ through Babbitt's mediumship. Rather, what he had contacted was what he believed to be the Christ Spirit, a "force of the spirit, a force of nature, a universal force, not limited to any religion."

When he and Babbitt spoke of Christ, Hapgood clarified, they were not speaking, statically, of a person, but of an energy, dynamically.

"But the consciousness is there, the Christ Consciousness," he wrote. "And it is the Christ Consciousness that speaks in this book."

In his own "open letter" to readers of their book, Elwood Babbitt expressed his wish that it be understood that he served merely as the channel for the messages of the Christ Spirit to the world, "not the author of their expressions."

Insisting that he claimed no "spiritual authority" and "no license to dispense final truth," Babbitt compared himself to "the surface of a quiet lake reflecting the sun" or to "a telephone seeking to serve."

In one session with Hapgood, the Christ Spirit defined itself as Master to those without spiritual awareness, those who worship his name, and those who truly seek spiritual understanding:

> . . . I am never far away. I am watching the charges that are mine. There comes into the world a sign from the heavens: There shall be much suffering and stress among humanity. For it is a necessity that they learn to revitalize and to reopen that spirituality that has been long dormant within them.
>
> Though I have the power to bring forth a new and better creation—and though I am the I AM, the Consciousness on High, still I retain that which is needed, not for the betterment of all concerned, but because through the lessons of a material existence the spiritualities of all have yet great lessons to learn.
>
> You ask yourself the question: "Why am I here?" and the restless spirit within you answers, "To open wide the door so that you may exist on higher and greater planes than now."

CHAPTER TWENTY-THREE

✠

Jesus Led Her into the Light of Higher Awareness

"I have had times of great Light and amazing visions when Mother Mary and Jesus the Christ came to me while I am conducting a healing session with a client," Brenda Montgomery, a visionary channel and spiritual healer from Los Osos, California told us. "I believe that such appearances and visions come to love and to heal, and those who see and feel their presence are always blessed."

Brenda feels particularly pleased when Jesus manifests for an unbelieving client. "This becomes a time of many tears and a total change of mind and/or lifestyle."

She explained that her form of energy healing employs sound and vibration in an effort to have her clients become as "selfless" as possible, "so that they may have a life-changing experience of Light." On those wonderful occasions when Jesus comes as the Three-in-One—Father, Son, Holy Spirit—Brenda feels so blessed that she is "almost consumed in the Light and unable to work. But the energy flows and the healing takes place, even though I am in a place of 'blessed awareness.' "

Brenda recalled the time when she was working with a client on the massage table and a great golden light in the shape of a man walked into the room and stood beside her at the head of the table. She became so consumed by a blissful, loving state of consciousness that it was all that she could do to continue the healing process and "let the energy run and the tears roll."

The client was also aware of the golden light and received an impression of a "being" that had entered the room.

"Do you recognize the being?" Brenda asked.

The reply was a tearful, "I think it is Jesus!"

"Yes," Brenda said, confirming her client's impression. "He has come to you in a way that you could recognize."

On another occasion, Brenda herself lay on the massage table, the recipient of a fellow healer's ministrations.

"Jesus entered the room and came through the healer, who was at my head," Brenda said. "He lay down over me, and as His body sank into mine, we become one. The healer removed her hands from my body and stated that the healing had taken place. Two other healers who were present said that they could see the golden being come into the room and become a part of me."

As Brenda recalled the incredible experience of at-one-ment with the Christ energy:

> I could not speak or move, but I reveled in the completely beautiful, warm, golden and white Light that was in me. A message clearly formed in my head as His words filled me with a perfect knowing of how I was to take care of myself from that time on—and how I was to remember the experience to share with others.
>
> (I have not shared this experience until now—a little over a year later.)
>
> I could feel His hands in my hands, and I could feel His heart in my heart. How wonderful! And I could feel His body in every inch of me—all the way to my toes!
>
> I could not speak. At that moment of connection with the All That Is, there could be no earthly words to describe it.

The three healers in the room with Brenda were wise enough to leave her alone until she could move again under her own control.

"I don't recall how long I lay there," she said. "When I finally opened my eyes, I saw that the other healers were sitting around me very quietly, waiting for me to regain waking consciousness. We didn't speak, only smiled at each other and cried. We all knew that the Light of Light had been there."

The experience of at-one-ment with the energy form of Jesus had come to bless Brenda at a very crucial time in her life.

"My life was in total change," she explained. "My

thirty-six-year marriage was over. My home was for sale. I was not in a good place physically or mentally, and yet Jesus was willing to give to me all of His energy and Light—and I could only say, 'Thank you!' "

Convinced that all was being orchestrated by Spirit, Brenda was able to sell her home and to find the right place to establish a new residence. Jesus even saw to it that she had a wonderful, longtime friend to join her in the new home so that she could make the transition smoothly.

"She and I both constantly say, 'Thank you, God, for directing us to this beautiful new place and for giving us so much. We are truly blessed!' " Brenda said.

"Life is moving on. We have found a church that is filling us so that we may offer back to God all that He has given us. And although I cannot fully explain any of this, I only know with my heart that I am still the recipient of that Holy Light as often as I need it. It is never refused! I just ask."

Brenda shared with us an earlier experience with the Light of Jesus, which occurred on November 11, 1991, near Awahanee, California. She and a number of others had been staying in an old farmhouse in anticipation of a spiritual event that had drawn people "from everywhere, it seemed."

Nancy, their hostess, had planned talks and other interesting activities, and everyone was free to wander on her farm and "smell the air at that altitude."

Brenda remembers that there was a bit of snow on the ground, "chilly outside, warm as toast inside," and that there was an atmosphere of expectancy, "of something wonderful in the wind."

Brenda said that she had been having "Kundalini experiences" all during this time of anticipation.

[In Hindu Tantra, "Kundalini" is the female energy within the body. It is often envisioned and represented in the form of a coiled serpent. Once awakened, the Kundalini moves up through the various *chakras* (energy centers) until it reaches the top of the head and brings about a state of blissful enlightenment.]

Yes, she had been having "Kundalini rumblings," but not enough, she thought, "to be worried about having an all-out Kundalini experience."

The final evening of the gathering, Nancy had planned with great care a circle of energy and Light. She stepped into the circle with four beautifully carved staffs and handed one to each person appointed to "hold" the energies of one of the four directions.

"She came straight to me with the staff that had the serpent dramatically carved on the top," Brenda said. "Nancy smiled at me as if to say, 'You need this—and this is the time.' "

Brenda felt the energy of the serpent churning in her first and second *chakras* (the base of the spine and the abdomen).

> I could barely stand up. I was shaking and my consciousness was in and out—yet I stood, holding the energy of the North with the staff of the serpent. The perspiration was pouring off my head, and the Kundalini was moving slowly, ever upwards. I didn't know what to do. I looked at Nancy with pure panic on my face, and she gave me a look that said, "You'll hold out until this is over."

Brenda thought that she would faint, but she just breathed deeply and asked God to help her get through it all.

At last the process was completed, and Nancy reclaimed the serpent staff.

"Just go to the back bedroom," she told Brenda. "Your massage table is already set up. Get on it, and we will assist you."

Somehow Brenda managed to get on the table and to lie down. And then she had a "full-out movement of the Kundalini."

> In this time and space, I cannot relate to you all that I saw . . . all that I felt . . . all that I was allowed to hear. But I can tell you this: It was painful.
>
> At times I would cry out to God to help me. I prayed for the ability to come through this with grace.
>
> There was not one minute of this time that I was not in the present. Even when I was seeing visions of things that I have never seen—and things that even now I cannot fully explain—even when I was talking to those who were there in Spirit to assist me, I was still fully conscious. This period lasted for about three hours.
>
> There were people around the table with their hands on me, trying to assist me, but the Kundalini is a very personal and private thing. When you are ready to move through it—or let it move through you—then no one can really help. But I felt so loved and so fortunate to have so many

friends see me through this intense episode of consciousness raising.

All at once my body relaxed. As if ten thousand lights had come on, I saw in front of me a huge vision that seemed to be as all-encompassing as the sky. It was as if it had been painted by one of the great masters. In its beauty, it was not unlike the ceiling of the Sistine Chapel.

There were Masters and teachers and angels moving all around me. And then I thought my heart would burst when I saw that the "main character" of this "enlightenment play" was the Christ Jesus. My Brother. My Savior. All the names that I had ever known to call Him came to me. And He spoke to me!

He said that I must relax and allow the energies to flow, that this experience was for my highest good. And it was good that the enlightenment had occurred when friends could witness it and be blessed by it—and when I could fully trust and be certain that I would be safe. I looked around me for a moment and saw my students, my friends, and people I didn't know, but I felt perfectly safe and secure.

In the middle of all this brightness and love, I remember thinking, "Could this be a fantasy?"

At that moment I was given a most beautiful and loving gift. From behind the robes of Jesus Christ I saw a little dark-haired girl peek out. I looked at her and began to cry.

It was little Vanessa, the daughter of my dear friends Terry and Kathy, who had made her transition at the age of twelve due to a terrible disease. I knew then that I must move through the rest of the process because it was the Truth. I had an awareness that Vanessa had been allowed to make herself known to me so that there would be no doubts left in my mind. And there she was, so full of life! And just as beautiful as she had always been.

And so the energies rolled on and a higher path was opened for Brenda.

When it was over, she was exhausted. So she slept.

"The next morning, when I could finally stand again, I ate some breakfast in a kind of daze," she recalled. "I was still feeling and seeing so much Light around the house and in everyone—and colors of such great hue and proportion.

"Everyone wanted to know about my experience, but the words just weren't there. This was a private and emotional transition into the Light of Light, with the evolving energies helping me onto the path of enlightenment. I thank God for giving me such a beautifully organized way of having this experience."

Brenda does have some words of advice for those who seek higher awareness:

We—you and I—are so blessed with so much Light. If the moment has not yet come for you, then ask! There is not one person who cannot ask for this wonderful comingling of the energy of the All That Is.

Turn up your love energy, and agree that any time you need that blessing of Light and Love that it may present itself to you. Fully know that this is Truth, and the Light shall come to you.

More and more often in this day and time, the Father, Jesus the Christ, the Three in One, will come, for He wants us to recognize His great love and His peace so that we can share it with everyone.

And I say, 'Thank you, Jesus, for being with me at all times. And thank you for coming to my assistance in my own healing and in the healing of others. You are my Light and Life and my only Source!'

CHAPTER TWENTY-FOUR

✠

She Joined Jesus on a Journey of Ascension

Liz Smith Anderson's journey began a few years ago when her friend, Beverly Hale Watson, began giving her Bibles, because she was instructed by Spirit to do so.

"I would tuck them away, not wanting to read them and not wanting to hurt Beverly's feelings," Liz confesses in her foreword to her book, *A Journey of Ascension.*

"I knew in my heart that Beverly was very connected to the Christ Consciousness, yet I was reluctant to read a document that did not seem to contain many truths for me. I also knew in my heart that the main message that Jesus came to impart to us was one of Ascension. He came to help prepare us for a new way of being, a new Earth. That message seems to be buried beneath the image of the God of punishment portrayed by many Christian denominations."

After Beverly gave her a second Bible, Liz (also known by her spiritual name of "Liberty") received a message from a high spirit being, who asked if she could not read the New Testament for her own growth. She replied that she supposed that she could do so, and the being added a shocking declaration:

> *As you read the Book, Jesus and the Apostles will work through you and bring forth the Truth of what and who the man Jesus was and is.*

The process took her two years and produced "many tears and a soul that has come full circle in the Love of God."

In personal correspondence to us, Liz/Liberty wrote: "This book was received entirely from the Higher Realms for the purpose of healing my emotional body with the Christian religions of this Earth."

She was supported both emotionally and financially by all the members of her meditation group. Without their support, her work would not have been completed. By working in oneness with each other, the process of healing was softened.

"It was during my time with this group that I learned to trust that God would provide the teacher when the student was ready."

Liz continues to be open and to receive spiritual information on a daily basis. "Spirit is part of who I am—and whether people know it or not, it is a part of them, too."

In the foreword to her book, Liz states that she has arrived at the place in her spiritual evolution where the concept of God has moved beyond gender:

> I see God as all that there is and all that will ever be . . . This does not mean that I do not love and

cherish the Father/Mother/Son, nor does it mean that I deny the existence of the Father or Mother or Son . . . I wish not to find truth for you, but to help you find your own truth.

A message from Jesus, excerpted from *A Journey of Ascension,* received by Liz Smith Anderson:

All who listen to my words shall know peace, love, and everlasting life.

I love all of humankind. Please listen to these words. They come from the heart and soul of the Universe. I thank all those who have listened to their Inner Voice and who have sought the truth about what is really happening on Earth. Others will be awakening soon.

Don't get caught up in holding true to the traditions of man. Hold true to the God-Self—and most of all to the Supreme Creative Force.

Love—The Most Powerful Force in Existence

Love! Love is the most powerful force in existence. It brings life, glory, health, and happiness. It is the binding and welding substance of souls. It is eternal, for physical death cannot destroy it.

Without love there is no unity or strength. It is imperative to love yourself, your parents, your spouse, your children, your neighbor—everyone! Love all creatures, great and small.

Belief in Contact with Jesus Constitutes a Saving Grace

I know that for many of you the fact that I, Jesus, am amongst you and that we can speak and feel each other is very foreign and unbelievable. Yet many on Earth have persisted in the belief that they can talk with me and that has been the saving grace for us here in the "heavens."

Many Are in Turmoil Over Matters of Faith

Many beings on Earth are in great turmoil over the very subjects of Faith, Spirituality, Religion, and God. People must not separate themselves from God to be with God, yet many, many religions do just that. They accuse "New Age" people of working with the devil. They try to make members of their faith fear God.

I come today to tell all who will listen that the "job descriptions" that many of you felt were valid may no longer be so, as we here are reassigning many of you. You have been moved from the "front lines" to a more secondary position—and there is a good reason for this. You may have been identified as being one with the devil, because some do not understand the Christ Consciousness. Many of you have been where they are. You have been lost, and now you have found your way back to God.

It may have been a long, hard climb for you; yet, as your knowledge and truth in God's love grew, you also grew to understand more of the Universal beingness that was housed inside the large body called humanity.

Most of you know so well that God is love. You must stand firm in your belief that God loves everyone and everyone is of God.

At-One-Ment Is for All Who Have God's Love in Their Hearts

Inside this body called humanity is a great variety of beingness, many levels of knowing—many roads to Rome, as it has been said. And many of you have realized that to become at-one with the Christ Consciousness is what one should strive towards. And this at-one-ment is for *all* who have the love of God in their hearts—not just for this group or that group, but for all.

There are those among you who will remain in the "front lines" of faith, so to speak. There are those who will change positions as the need arises. There are those who will never be recognized for their contributions, yet they will keep going, no matter what.

It Is Not for Any Human to Judge Another's Service

It is not for any human to judge the work of another, for all serve God. If you can pass through the illusion called life on Earth and remember that all are from One Source, then you will have succeeded in your earthly task. All beings are of the Universal Substance called Love. Those who have placed God in the position of being an unreachable goal have limited themselves in the reality of what can and cannot be. There is nothing that cannot be if you allow it to be.

Remember the goal of the God Being: To reconnect with all of Its aspects incarnate everywhere, in every universe.

The Principal Goal of Humankind Is to Go Home to God

Your principal goal should be to go home to God. You cannot accomplish Ascension through me, Jesus. You must accomplish this goal through your own spirit, which is part and parcel of God and will always be of God.

Let yourself feel the eternal connection within your being. The heart connection that for so long has been weak and faint can be revitalized through Faith, Peace, and Love of God. (And therefore yourself!) Know that God is within you and that you humans, as a species, can ascend to Heaven on Earth.

It is up to you now to create this Heaven. I am here to help by loving and supporting each of you. You must give the love!

I love you ALL, *Jesus*

CHAPTER TWENTY-FIVE

✠

A Message from Jesus Regarding the New Energies Manifesting Today on Earth

As received by Brenda Montgomery, who asked for words of love or guidance to be given especially for this book:

Dearest Sisters and Brothers, I AM ready to give you a message of the times from the heart of my Father.

We do sign these writings as Jesus the Christ or John Immanuel or Your Brother . . . as is the energy of this channel, Brenda, at the time; so we will bring the correct energy to her. There are times when she accepts no other name than my name [Jesus], but she also understands that when the message is going out to a particular individual . . . that person may not be able to accept the actual name as being the Truth—so we, in essence, soften the name by signing a simple name so that the Truth may be given and accepted.

These are difficult times, but very high energy times; and all those who need their questions answered may have the Truth given to them as needed . . . We shall offer words that are needed—and so it is!

The Present Day Offers Enlightenment Opportunities for All

Many times in the earthly flow, there has been a need for us to come to the aid of those we feel are becoming lost in the haze; that is, those who are falling by the wayside by not seeing the Light.

In this present day, there those who, so deeply feeling the energy of the times, are fighting to stay afloat, and we must come to their rescue. This has happened many times in what you would call a day, and we take these occurrences very seriously.

The present time is proving to be a great and enlightening treat for a few—but for the many these are horrible times of change. While there are words of good being uttered, there is simply not enough power being put into them.

This is an enlightened time of beauty for each of you, and you may choose to come into enlightenment if you so wish and if your path has brought you into the study and the prayer that these things require. Many are finding the path of Light, but there are too many who do not believe—or understand—the path. There are those who openly ridicule and "put down" the "New Age" movement as being pap or nonsense, meaningless words spoken to deflect the new ways from the "church" as they know it.

It Is Time for People to Declare the Path of Light and Oneness

People on Earth, it is time to declare your Light and follow the path of Oneness. It is not time to use trivial words to change the old ways, but begin anew!

New thought, new light, there are so many new meanings to the word, "enlightenment." These present times are packed with new energies, we cannot understand why the many of you are not totally involved with, and caring for, the work of Light.

It is time, my Sisters and Brothers. It is time to begin again with a new kind of meditation—but only if you are going to put your full energy into moving into the place of Oneness. It is essential that you do this. Every time you close your energy and ask for meditation, let your heart draw the Light of my Father's love and begin to feel the energies flow through you.

Accept New Energies in this Time of Empowerment

This is a powerful time. Allow yourself to become a part of the new energies.

Too many of you seem to feel that you need lessons in how to change, lessons in how to use this new energy. No! All you have to do is breathe, breathe the breath of Life and feel yourself fill with the new energy.

If you so say that you have breathed in the new energy, then you shall feel it. If you do not proclaim the new energies and new times, you shall fail to find the way.

Your affirmation of the new *is* the way.

Finding the words of your Truth *is* the way.

Feel for yourself the change within as you proclaim new energy.

Breathe and feel as you are so filled. The energy is new—and it is that which you need to flow into the ascension time. Your hearts will be blessed and healed by this new Light energy.

It is possible now to fill yourself and then ask for what you so desire. If it should be enlightenment, ask for it to come to you—and you will receive it in the way that you are to have it.

All Those Who Truly Seek Enlightenment Must Do Their Work

For those of you who came in to pray for enlightenment through psychic receivership, then you must do your work. For those of you who chose the way of Christian ethics or Hebrew studies or the many and varied other religious paths, pray without ceasing, and ask for my Father's guidance. You shall be enlightened in your hearts and minds.

I say this, when it is time for you to receive enlightenment, there will be many changes in your life as you now know it. You must work through these changes.

Some will say to themselves, "I cannot go through this! It is too difficult!" And they will not be moved to change.

If you so desire to have enlightenment on the Earth plane, then you must do the work required. If you ask for this holy theme, you will be given the way. You will know what it is that you have to do.

Understand, dear ones, that there is no gift of enlightenment that you can have if you do not work for it. Times have not changed so much that you will not be required to work for your enlightenment. What is not worked for, is not worth having.

Pray Without Ceasing to Receive the Riches of Enlightenment

Prayer is a way. Prayer is required regardless of which path you may be on. Things have not changed so that prayer has been excluded as a requirement.

Pray without ceasing to receive the richness of life through enlightenment.

Loving Sisters and Brothers, I yearn for your desire to be of holy and Light ways and that your path be secured with Light. I wish that you hold dear to the ways of your Masters and Teachers.

You have so many Masters on Earth now. Use their information. Feel their blessings of Light. Even though they are of earthly bodies, there is a Light within them that can help you to find your own path.

Recognize the Masters of Earth by Their Peace and Light

The Masters of Earth are there for you. You will know them by their peace and Light. You will sense their inner knowings, and you will desire to be near them.

Trust with all your heart that there are earthly Masters who will heed your words and deliver unto you the Truth. Search and you shall find them. Pray, and they shall be revealed to you.

Brothers and Sisters of Earth, come now into a great time of prayer. Seek to pray with those with whom you work, with friends, with family. Pray alone in the silence of your home, pray to the heavens as you explore the beauty of Earth. Pray in the peace of your favorite holy place.

The earthly Masters will help you to discover a way to pray fully, with passion and simplicity.

Prayer can be your way to allow each person who comes in touch with you to feel your Light.

It is of the utmost importance that you seek to work toward a prayerful manner of living. If all humans could discover the many ways of prayerful playing, as well as working, life could come close to peace on Earth.

The Beauty of the Prayerful Way

The beauty of the prayerful way is that it leads to happiness and security in the earthly life—and happiness and security in the next life. The prayerful way constitutes a powerful and loving way to live.

Be at peace, my Sisters and Brothers, you are about to enter a time of blessed being and powerful love.

The theme of these new times must be prayer. Look at the skies—and deliver a brief prayer. Look at the waters of Earth—and send a brief prayer. Listen to the music of Earth—and say a prayer of thanks. Your way should be thankfulness for everything—including your next breath.

Peace to you now as I take my leave. My friends, my Brothers and Sisters, we are one; and we are all One with my Father. Seek through prayer and find your true Light.

Peace be with you now,

Your Brother, Jesus the Christ, the Three in One, God the Father

CHAPTER TWENTY-SIX

✠

An Exercise from Jesus on Grounding the Ascension Energies

As received by Brenda Montgomery, "from Jesus Christ, my Light and my Heart":

Jesus Begins the Process by Opening the Chakras

As you go through this meditation, you will be opening each chakra [the physical body's energy centers] to the fullest. Be prepared for this opening process by knowing in your heart that if you are supposed to receive these energies, then you will be safe and secure with the chakras fully open. Do not be afraid to open fully.

This is your chance to have the Ascension Energies completely in and through you so that you are ready for whatever is to come. The highest and most loving guidance will be with you as you work your way to total openness.

As you proceed through this meditation process, feel each chakra in its own beautiful light. Allow it to be any color you see there. Let the Light blaze out to fill your body, your room, your area, your world, your universe!

Use in-breaths to expand each chakra more and more—and keep your breath free and alive! Use your hands to touch the chakra areas and sweep outward in an expanding way. Feel an openness, even a vulnerability there, as well as life and emotion.

As you come to the end of instruction for each chakra, it is up to you to feel the results of your prayer and to visualize the energies coming forth from the heavens, pouring down in a column of light as wide as your body and filling each chakra one by one. Your visualization of the process will make it seem more real to you, and we will help you by supplying the love that is yours to have.

So let us begin by opening each chakra:

FIRST CHAKRA: **At the base of your spine** feel your groundedness even more clearly now, for all the energies will flow through this open chakra.

Say to yourself—

> "I **am** safe on Earth. I **am** abundantly provided for by God and the Universe. The Earth holds me now, and it is pleasurable beyond belief to be opening fully my first chakra! **I am that I am."**

SECOND CHAKRA: **Sensing your second chakra in your abdomen** say—

"I **am** centered. I **am** safe and loved and expressing my sexuality and creativity, which is welcome in the world. My sexuality is Divine Energy, and God approves of it. My second chakra is expanding now, fully opening to all the Light that will bring me home at that wonderful time. I feel the column of heavenly Light pouring through me now."

THIRD CHAKRA: **Feel your solar plexus** flooding with angelic, holy Light, and say—

"For the first time, my third chakra is cleared and balanced. I am safe and loved in expressing my own power and creativity. My power and my creative ways, together with myself as spirit and love, are one. The third chakra is expanded and the Light is pouring through it now!"

FOURTH CHAKRA: As the Light column now gently enters **your heart chakra,** say—

"For the first time I feel my heart center as the great Light of love that it is. I am safe and full of love as never before, and I am loved without limit. I know that the **I Am** love is my guidance. All love is with me now. Blessed be."

FIFTH CHAKRA: As the Light explodes in **your thymus chakra,** you feel as you have never felt before because the opening of this chakra brings purity and total oneness. Say—

"In that space between my heart and throat there is a great Light, and I am blessed. My new chakra is fully functioning in order to give me the power of cleansing and the ability to open to new adventures of the heart and throat energies. It is fully open now! I see the mighty colors of change!"

SIXTH CHAKRA: Your **throat center** is now filled with the column of Light. Say—

"I am fully open to expressing my light, my path, and my oneness with the All That Is. I am safe and loved in expressing my truth, my power, and my passion. I am full and free and receiving. I **am** abundance, and my throat chakra is fully open now."

SEVENTH CHAKRA: The magenta chakra **at the base of your skull** now pulsates with the column of Light. Say—

"The magenta color encapsulates me now, and I feel as I have felt before the promise of the Zeal Point chakra. It pulls the violet of the spiritual chakra and the red of base chakra to blend into a full and balanced center of truth that opens me to the Oneness and creates a powerful spiritual center of clarity and peace. The beautiful magenta is my perfect knowing that I am now clearly open to All That Is."

EIGHTH CHAKRA: The Third Eye, **between your eyebrows,** is now filling with the column of Light. Say—

"I **am** safe and loved, and I **am** in the Light of Knowledge that permits me to know everything that I need to know. Let the indigo chakra be opened and widened by the column of Light that is now present. Let me see all that I have not seen before."

NINTH CHAKRA: **The crown chakra at the top of your head** is filling with the column of Light. Say—

"I am safe and loved. I **am** an unlimited being present in all universes. I **am** open in this pure white light center now. I feel the column of holy light stretching my crown chakra to the limits. Praise heaven!"

TENTH CHAKRA: Visualize this chakra **above your head** and let the column of white Light expand and elevate you. Say—

"I **am** loved to the fullest, and I am totally safe when I step in peace through the dimensions of spirituality. I **am** open and clear in my tenth chakra now."

ELEVENTH AND TWELFTH CHAKRAS: Visualize these chakras **in the space immediately above your tenth chakra** and see them open to the whole universe. Say—

"I **am** safe and blessed and loved in this open state of being. I am ready to make my ascension when it is time, for I can feel that it is safe and real. All my chakras are open for the final experience that I am to have—whether it be here or on the other side. I am open to being guided or to be the guide.

"I will do for God what He is now doing for me. My life is at its fullest, and my tears are for the ones who may not experience this heavenly blessing.

"My promise is that I will share this meditation process with others and grant them the security of knowing fully who they are in the Light of all Light."

Grounding the Ascension Energies

Now with perfect intention, visualize the sky opening up and the Light beginning to pour down. The angels and the beautiful guidance from heaven are directing the flow of the Light. You can clearly see the beautiful Ascension Energies pouring downward in many shades of color, more vibrant than a rainbow, and sprinkled with gold.

As the pure Ascension Energies come down toward you, there is a marvelous feeling in your body and mind. You can feel the flow of energy begin to enter your fully expanded chakras.

As the energy pours through you, each chakra is cleansed and purified. You feel as though you are being transformed from mere earthly being into a purified being on Earth. You feel at once a part of Earth and a part of Spirit.

As the energies flow through the highest chakras, you can barely remain centered, but you know that you can only become one with these Ascension Energies if you stay clear and feel the transition. Oh, the Light that flows through you is so marvelous, so blessed!

Now sense the feeling of peace as the energies move down through the top of your head and enter your crown and third-eye chakras. You had never expected to experience such a perfect, rarified peace on Earth. It is as if you are in a heavenly state.

The Ascension Energies begin to move through the Zeal Point chakra, and as they do, there is a burst of magenta into the energies as they meld in a perfection of feeling and knowing—a true blending of the spiritual and the earthly.

The energies meld with the blue of the throat, and you are overwhelmed by words that have needed to be expressed. Know that they will come to you when you need them after you have completed this meditation process. Certain of the word-thoughts that you are feeling have never been heard before. They will be so truly spiritual and blessed.

The Ascension Energies move down into your heart, the fourth chakra. You may now be thinking, "Oh, Father, the blessings that you have given me and the pure love that is mine, how can I fully understand this blessing?"

Dear ones, you can! You are being given the highest and most loving light available—and it is blessing your body and soul now. Let your heart feel its full glory and sing! Expand the green color of the heart into the beautiful energies of the ascension.

As the energies begin to pour into the third chakra, the solar plexus with its color of yellow, you experience a new understanding of creativity. Your body vibrates so powerfully with this new awareness that you nearly lose your balance and feel as though you might faint.

Take a deep breath and stay with this flow! Don't permit the earthly you to ruin your opportunity to experience the glorious light of the Ascension Energies. Feel the powerful new you merge with the energies as they meld with the yellow energy center of creativity.

Now the Ascension Energies begin to fill the orange color of the second chakra with peace, and you are truly blessed by this grounding process. Flow with the gold-tinged rainbow Light and allow your physical body to really **feel** for the first time.

Your red center at the base of your spine opens to the rarified Ascension Energies, and all the colors flowing through you are made brighter. There is music in the ethers. The angels sing. And you are finally fully aligned in truth, peace, and oneness.

Whatever you need to express to your guides, to your teachers, to God, do it now.

"Thank you" is hardly enough, for you have been filled as never before—and you have become a part of the precious Ascension Energies! You have now breathed the ethers of heaven. You have become beautiful Beings of Light. You are one with God!

Now permit the Light to move on as Mother Earth opens herself to the Light of Light.

There is a moment of breathlessness as the Oneness of Heaven to Earth is made complete. **We have the Ascension Energies fully flowing now!** Praise God!

You now have the peace that could never before be understood. You now know your future, and you now stand fully ready to move forward in the directions that your respective paths need to express. This is a gift of love so great! Open your hearts even more and give back your thanks to your angelic guides and to God.

You now know that living with the Ascension Energies can bring you more peace than you have ever had before. You know now that whatever you choose to do in the future, you will be blessed—and you will bless others with your new Light and understanding.

It matters not who you are or what color you are or what your earthly heritage may be. You have Heaven on Earth when you use this meditation process.

Now, Dear Ones, very slowly permit the energies to rise back up and allow your chakras to relax fully. Do allow them to remain in a fully balanced state as long as you can, for this is peace as you have never before experienced it. This is love at its fullest.

Know that you may call upon the Ascension Energies whenever you need them and understand that they are available to keep you centered in your spiritual work on Earth. You may use them to clear and to heal yourselves and others; but most of all, the Ascension Energies are to help those of you on Earth to be able to do fully the work of God.

Blessings to each of you on your individual paths—and blessings to each of you for your ability to clear your centers and to hold this new Light. You are now ready for whatever may occur on Earth.

Blessings and Peace,

Your Brother, Jesus Christ

CHAPTER TWENTY-SEVEN

Summoning the Light Within

Susanne B. Miller of Santa Fe, New Mexico, uses a technique she calls "clairaudient meditation" to conduct inspirational conversations with those who now exist in the Higher Realms. In answer to our correspondence, she told us that she has always believed that the purpose of each individual is to achieve full soul expression in order to discover and to manifest one's divine mission.

"It seems that the legacy that Jesus left was one of demonstrating this—and letting everyone know that they too are capable of the same feats, and more," she said.

During the 1980s, Susanne exerted great effort toward getting in touch with inner worlds.

"I called upon my higher self and spiritual guides

to lead me in the right direction. So it seemed completely natural when I started to receive messages from Jesus."

Susanne, who happens to be Jewish, is another of those ecumenical mystics who allow no religious dogma to inhibit their contact with inner and outer worlds of awareness.

"The words of Jesus," she continued, "were always comforting and uplifting. In 1994, I channeled a booklet entitled *Summon the Light Within: Daily Exercises and Meditations with Master Jesus.* I knew that I was being asked to spread his words of peace and joy to those who were willing to accept his essence."

More recently, in 1997, Susanne channeled another book, *Interviews with Famous Dead People: Inspirational Conversations,* in which Jesus, along with Mother Mary, granted her an interview.

"One of the things that Jesus reminds us about is the Second Coming, which I find particularly appropriate during these tumultuous times. He and Mother Mary make a distinction between the Christian belief that Jesus will manifest in the physical and the alternate teaching that his return must occur within our hearts."

According to Jesus:

> Before I incarnated upon the Earth nearly 2,000 years ago, I decided that as the man Jesus, I would spend that life raising my vibration in order to become Christed—at One with God . . . Through much work, faith, and devotion, I was able to achieve my aim . . . I was sent as an example to demonstrate that each of you also has the ability to raise your God-awareness and vitality as I have

done in order to achieve the Christed state. "You will do what I have done, and greater still."

Therefore, what is referred to as the Second Coming is not, as so many falsely believe, my return in a physical form—although many of you will be able to perceive me as such—but rather my Christed nature appearing within each and every one of you . . .

Mother Mary, as channeled by Susanne Miller, states that the Second Coming is "the recognition of the Christ spirit within all of us, not outside of us, nor within a selected few."

Susanne said that she was saddened by the fact that it has taken over two thousand years for humanity to assimilate the actual truths that Jesus represented.

"It has been my experience that this powerful being nurtures and supports everyone in whatever capacity they are willing to accept him," she commented.

"Once we truly receive Jesus' essence into our hearts, we'll recognize that he is always there and always has been. He is a great example toward which we might all aspire."

Here, with Susanne's permission is an exercise in forgiveness excerpted from her booklet, *Summon the Light Within: Daily Exercises and Meditations with Master Jesus:*

Forgiveness is for Giving: A Circle of Joy

Forgiveness is the art of letting go. The time has come for you to eliminate the impurities that you have accumulated. The time is now.

Before we begin this exercise, I would like to discuss the importance of forgiveness. Perhaps there were times in your life when you wronged another. You may have attempted to slow down or stop their life flow.

On the other hand, there may have been times when the tables were turned and it was you who became the so-called victim. I am telling you now that the latter is a result of the former when forgiveness is not utilized.

What I just described regarding forgiveness is, of course, karma—the law of cause and effect. Forgiveness can be applied to ease the burden of karma. This exercise is designed to aid you in this process. But when doing this exercise, remember that in order to make it work, it must come from your heart—not from your head.

Close your eyes and relax. Take a few deep breaths. Be sure to inhale through your nose and exhale through your mouth. This will help you to become even more relaxed and centered.

Now visualize a golden light—the *Light of Forgiveness.* It is here to aid you.

Recall an incident when you did not act appropriately toward someone else or they toward you. Surround that person—and the incident—with this golden light. Hold that vision . . . love that vision . . and say to yourself three times:

I AM Forgiveness acting now!

Hold what you are forgiving a little longer in the golden light—then let it go. Know that once you let it go, it is banished into the light forever.

Next visualize the golden light encircling Earth. Realize that this beautiful, forgiving energy is penetrating Her and all of Her inhabitants. Then bring the light back around yourself and experience the joy that has come from balancing your karma.

Give your full attention to only one forgiveness incident at a time. This is the best way to balance each episode that has occurred in this lifetime that requires forgiveness.

Be honest with yourself, for this is the only way this exercise can work properly . . . Enjoy!

CHAPTER TWENTY-EIGHT

✠

Lord, Teach Us How to Pray

And it came to pass while he was praying in a certain place, when he finished, one of his disciples said to him, Our Lord, teach us to pray . . .

Jesus said to them, When you pray, pray like this, Our Father in heaven, Hallowed be thy name. Thy Kingdom come. Thy will be done, as in heaven, so on earth.

Give us bread for our needs every day.

And forgive us our sins, for we have also forgiven all who have offended us. And do not let us enter into temptation; but deliver us from error (anything contrary to the truth; evil).

[Luke 11:1–4; George M. Lamsa's translation from the Aramaic]

The authors of this book have always sought to practice the advice concerning prayer that St. Paul gives in I Thessalonians ("Pray without ceasing"), and we are both firm believers in the power of prayer.

Throughout the gospels, Jesus himself prayed a great deal. In addition to his giving of the well-known "Lord's Prayer" in Luke, as quoted above, Jesus prayed at his baptism (Luke 3:21), before he chose the Twelve (Luke 6:12), before his invitation to all humankind to "come unto" him (Matthew 11:25–27), at the feeding of the five thousand (John 6:11), before his Transfiguration (Luke 9:28–29), for little children (Matthew 19:13), at the Last Supper (Matthew 26: 26–27), for Peter (Luke 22:32), in Gethsemane (Matthew 26:36–44), and on the Cross (Luke 24:30), to name only some of the more significant prayers recorded by the gospel writers.

We feel strongly that Jesus encouraged spontaneous prayers spoken from the heart, rather than memorized, all-purpose, canned prayers for any occasions. God, the Source of All-That-Is, wants to know what is truly in the depths of our own souls, not to hear how well we can recite the poetic or ponderous thoughts of a learned theologian.

"Prayer is not eloquence, but earnestness," wrote English author Hannah More. "Prayer is not the definition of helplessness, but the feeling of it. Prayer is not figures of speech, but earnestness of soul."

Concerning the Lord's Prayer

The Lord's Prayer has long been esteemed as containing the sum total of religion and morals.

"The Lord's Prayer, for a succession of solemn

thoughts, for fixing the attention upon a few great points, for suitableness to every condition, for sufficiency for conciseness without obscurity, for the weight and real importance of its petition, is without equal or a rival," according to William Paley, an eighteenth-century British theologian.

Before Paley had declared the Lord's Prayer as a peerless series of petitions, seventeenth-century Bishop Jeremy Taylor had written: "The Lord's Prayer is short and mysterious, and, like the treasures of the Spirit, full of wisdom and latent senses."

English cleric John Frederick Dennison Maurice, however, cautioned that the Lord's Prayer "is not, as some fancy, the easiest, the most natural of all devout utterances. It may be quickly committed to memory, but it is slowly learned by heart."

We do not wish in any way to demean the power of the Lord's Prayer, but we feel quite certain that when Jesus was asked by his disciples to teach them how to pray, he intended the form of the Lord's Prayer to be used only as a kind of outline, a guide to the creating of a proper approach to God, together with a number of suggestions for suitable kinds of petitions to be included in respectful prayers. We doubt very much if Jesus intended the prayer to be uttered in unison in religious services throughout all of human history.

We firmly believe that Jesus prizes the inspiration of the individual heart above the form of a prayer that he issued strictly for his disciples to use as a model by which to fashion their own prayerful utterances.

The most effective prayers may indeed be our cries of pain and sorrow.

"Prayer," said St. Jerome *circa* 386, "is a groan."

Hundreds of years later, Madame Swetchine, a nineteenth-century Russian mystic, added, "Ah! Our groans are prayers as well. The very cry of distress is an involuntary appeal to that invisible Power whose aid the soul invokes."

Pray in Secret

While we both believe firmly that prayer can work mysteries and miracles, we are also very sensitive to the admonitions that Jesus pronounced concerning the secret nature of the act of praying.

> And when you pray, do not be like the hypocrites, who like to pray, standing in the synagogues and at the street corners, so that they may be seen by men . . . When you pray, enter into your inner chamber and lock your door, and pray to your Father who is in secret, and your Father who sees in secret shall himself reward you openly.
>
> And when you pray, do not repeat your words like the pagans, for they think that because of much talking they will be heard.
>
> Do not be like them, for your Father knows what you need before you ask him.
>
> (Matthew 6:5–8. George M. Lamsa's translation from the Aramaic.)

Bible scholar Henry H. Halley, commenting on Jesus' emphasis on secret prayer, states:

> We should never be ashamed to pray, or to give our testimony to our faith in prayer, as occasion may demand. But we should be on our guard lest

our thought is what impression we are making on the people. Prayer is the expression of ourself to God. It is a matter between ourselves and God; not something to talk about. By far the larger part of our prayer life should be absolutely secret, so as to give ourselves no chance to fool ourselves on our motives.

SECRETS FOR SUCCESSFUL PRAYERS

Harold Sherman, author–screenwriter–playwright–novelist and renowned psychic-sensitive, received international attention in 1937 when the Russian aviator Sigismund Levanevsky and his five-man crew vanished while on a daring flight over the polar regions. The Soviet government prevailed on the famous British Arctic explorer Sir Hubert Wilkins to conduct a search for the missing airmen; just before Sir Hubert left on his mission, he had lunch with Sherman, during which the two men agreed to attempt to remain in telepathic contact with each other.

Amazingly, Sherman was able to determine the location of the expedition, the events that Sir Hubert observed, and the mechanical difficulties that the explorer was having with the plane that he flew. Reginald Iverson, who had been hired by *The New York Times* to keep in radio contact with Sir Hubert's search party, found that sunspot and magnetic conditions had made regular communication impossible, and he had been able to get through to Sir Hubert on only a very few occasions. In an affidavit, Iverson testified that Sherman had been able to receive more accurate knowledge via telepathy with Sir Hubert than he had been able to gain from his sporadic radio contact with the expedition.

For the rest of his long and fruitful life, Harold Sherman worked tirelessly to devote his spiritual energies toward helping ordinary men and women develop the same mental powers that had enabled him to maintain telepathic contact with an Arctic explorer halfway around the world.

In 1970, when Brad Steiger met Harold Sherman, he remembers talking excitedly about his admiration for the famous sensitive until Sherman finally laughed, turned to his wife, and said, "Martha, this man knows more about me than I do!"

Their friendship led to many delightful and insightful conversations that went on for hours at a time. Brad came to know Harold Sherman as a wise, gentle, extremely devout man, who always spoke in a down-to-earth, straightforward manner about spiritual matters.

The Act of Prayer Is an Individual Proposition

Sherman always said that prayer, rightly understood and exercised, can lead every sincere seeker to a more direct and knowing communication with God.

However, the act of prayer, he firmly believed, is distinctly an individual proposition. Each of us must find God in his or her own way.

"The only Source that you ever need to reach and impress is the God Presence within you," he said. "When this relationship is knowingly established on a day-to-day basis, you will be the recipient of new inspiration, guidance, and protection far beyond your ordinary human capacity. But you must be willing to take the time to prepare your mind for this great spiritual adventure."

Free the Mind of Fears and Doubts

Sherman made a point of telling his audiences that bringing about successful prayer in their lives demanded that they learn to make their minds clear channels.

If they allowed their minds to be filled with fears and doubts, it would not be possible for them to relax, to make themselves receptive, and to exercise the degree of faith required to accomplish effective prayer.

Prayer Must Never Be Considered a Duty or an Obligation

Sherman was also firm in stating that we should never pray as "a duty, an obligation, or a habit."

"We've all seen people who make a ritual of getting a prayer over with as quickly as possible," he said. "Such rapidly mumbled prayers have no thought or feeling behind them. Nothing is accomplished by such prayers."

Pray with Feeling, Not Mere Words

Over and over Harold Sherman stressed that it was the *feeling* behind a prayer, not the *words* thought or spoken, which gets through to God, to the Cosmic Consciousness level of mind.

"You actually pray every time you have a deep

desire for something—a strong yearning—whether you put it into words or not," he said.

And then he would remind his listeners of the admonition of Jesus when he delivered the Sermon on the Mount: "When ye pray, use not vain repetitions . . . for your Father knoweth what things ye have need of, before ye ask Him."

Why Some Prayers May Not Receive Answers

In his book, *How to Solve Mysteries of Your Mind and Soul,* Harold offered the following suggestions, which might explain why a proper prayer-connection was not being made to the God Power:

- There may be a lack of faith that what is being prayed for can and will be realized.
- Perhaps the supplicant has failed to make his or her mind a clear channel so that the God Power is able to work through it.
- The supplicant may be permitting conflicts to arise in his or her mind due to fears, resentments, or doubts.
- There is an insufficient amount of power of feeling behind the prayers.
- The prayers are for something impossible to attain—or for something undeserved.

Harold Sherman's Seven Secrets for Successful Prayer

ONE: Remove all fears and doubts from your mind before you start to pray.

TWO: Make your mind receptive so it is prepared to receive guidance and inspiration from the God Power within.

THREE: Picture clearly in your mind what it is that you desire to bring to pass in your life.

FOUR: Have unfaltering faith that with God's help what you are picturing will come true.

FIVE: Repeat your visualization and your prayer every night until what you have pictured becomes a reality.

SIX: Review each day's activities and constantly strive to improve your mental attitude, so your mind can become a clearer channel attuned to the God Power within.

SEVEN: Realize that if your thinking is right and if you persist with faith and put forth every effort in support of your prayer, then that which you create in your mind must eventually come to pass.

SIR ALISTER HARDY'S SCIENTIFIC EXPERIMENTS WITH PRAYER

Sir Alister Hardy was convinced that if we were to apply the scientific experimental method to theology, "we could have a new flowering of faith that could reshape our civilization." It was his contention that one can test the power of prayer, experimenting with it to see if it really works.

In his *Divine Flame,* Sir Alister outlines a method that he is certain will bring positive results if used in the right way. He admits that he is adapting the Lord's Prayer and the method that Jesus used in suggesting that one approach God as if one were truly His child and speaking to a beloved Father.

Perhaps, he concedes to his contemporary audience, "the form of this relationship is almost certainly a psychological one based upon one's own former filial affection." Although one knows the reality of one's relationship to the Godhead must be something very different than that of child to parent, Sir Alister explains, the visualization of God as a person enables one to have the emotional sense of devotion that is a necessary part of the process. "The analogy, if you like, sets up the relationship with this element beyond the conscious self."

Once the proper relationship has been established, Sir Alister set forth the following experiment to "test" the efficacy of prayer:

> Ask in all humility to receive help in trying to bring about a better state of the world [in Jesus' words: "Thy Kingdom come, Thy will be done"] and think in what ways one might oneself do something to this end.
>
> Ask to be shown how one can keep oneself in better health to play a better and more active part in the world. Ask oneself if one is abusing one's body by taking more than one's proper share of daily bread.
>
> Ask that we might realize our own faults and how to mend them, and how to forgive those who have trespassed against us.

> Ask that we may recognize with thought what are the real temptations and evils that are making our lives less worthy than they could be.

Sir Alister fully believed that if people were to carry out this experiment with deep feeling and devotion—and not simply rattle the prayer through in a matter of seconds as if it were a magical incantation—they will come to feel a new power in themselves, and feel in touch with a *power* and a *glory* beyond themselves, "which can make the world a different place, a new kingdom."

CHAPTER TWENTY-NINE

✠

Meeting Jesus on the Other Side

Thirty-four-year-old Rick Kremer had somehow managed to become separated from his friends when they were deer hunting in northwest Iowa in December 1995.

"You think of Iowa as a bunch of interconnected farms, cornfields, and friendly little towns, but in certain areas of the state there are still a lot of woods and places where someone unfamiliar with the countryside can get lost," Rick told us in the account that he had attached to his questionnaire. "And after two or three hours of hopelessly searching for my friends, I realized that I was thoroughly lost and confused.

"The temperature dropped well below zero when the sun went down, and I figured the wind-chill factor was at least twenty below. I didn't even have any matches with me to light a fire. It was my first time ever deer hunting, and I had really relied totally on my more experienced friends to provide all the essentials for survival in the field."

Earlier that day, he had fired most of his shells in a attempt to attract the attention of his buddies, Ike, Bill, and Paul. He tried firing one of his last twelve-gauge, solid-slug shotgun shells into a pile of leaves and sticks, hoping that the muzzle blast would ignite the dry tinder, but he only succeeded in scattering the would-be bonfire into the wind.

"I leaned back against a tree and started to pray," Kremer continued. "I had always been pretty religious, even after my confirmation. But lately, with marriage and work and three kids, I had become more or less an Easter and Christmas Christian. But I always prayed and felt right with Jesus, regardless of whether or not I was a regular churchgoer."

The last time Rick glanced at the luminous dial on his wristwatch, it was nearly ten o'clock. He had been out in the field since early morning. He felt himself growing numb with cold. His hooded parka and insulated coveralls had kept him plenty warm while he had been hiking through freshly fallen snow in the bright sunlight, but now he felt as though he could hardly move.

"Then I started getting really sleepy. I knew that I should stay awake and jump around to keep warm, but I started to feel real groggy and tired. I was soon feeling almost indifferent to my dangerous situation. I was drifting into what they call the 'sleep of the snows.' I was freezing to death."

Although Rick Kremer had always been highly skeptical of accounts of out-of-body and near-death experiences, he testified in his report that he suddenly felt as though he had left his physical body and was standing a short distance away viewing his frozen corpse.

"I looked terrible, leaning against that tree all hunched over. My normally ruddy complexion was ashen. My beard was covered with ice particles. I looked like Jack Frost."

Rick said that he next experienced the tunnel effect that so many near-death survivors have reported.

"I seemed to be moving down this dark tunnel. Up ahead I could see a brilliant light, so I kept moving toward it."

After an undetermined length of time, Rick said that he seemed to step into the light and emerge into a beautiful garden and bright sunshine.

"It reminded me of a garden that my Aunt Glenda used to have on their farm in southern Iowa. She used to fuss so over her plants, and she always had more kinds of beautiful flowers than anyone else I have ever known. This was like Aunt Glenda's garden in mid-June—only even more so."

After a few moments of luxuriating in the lovely flower garden, Rick said that he became aware of another presence that was standing off to his side.

"At first I couldn't believe my eyes! It was Jesus himself. He looked just the way that he did in the mural above the altar back in my old home church. He had shoulder-length, reddish-brown hair and beard, and he was dressed in a white gown with a blue hood or mantle over his shoulders. He was smiling at me, and I felt tears come to my eyes. I knew that I was in spirit, but I still felt like crying when I saw Jesus face-to-face.

"Then I thought about that old hymn that we used to sing about coming to the garden when the dew was still on the roses and then seeing that Jesus was also there and walking and talking with him. I don't actually remember seeing his lips move, but I heard his words inside me.

" 'Some day,' he told me, 'you will come home again to this garden and be with me in my kingdom. But your time is not yet now. You must go back and be a good person and a solid husband and a loving father.' "

Rick remembered that Jesus bade him to look into a still pond in the garden.

"On the surface of the water I could see my buddies heading in the direction of my body, just as if I was seeing it all happen in some kind of movie screen. My thoughts were kind of mixed. I certainly wanted to return to life and be with Judy and the kids, but I also felt so peaceful and at home with Jesus in the garden."

As Jesus and he watched the search from the strange vantage point of the pool in the garden, Rick saw Ike open his mouth to shout out his grim discovery when his flashlight beam fell upon the severely chilled body of his friend.

"I couldn't hear anything that any of them said, but I could see Ike yelling and waving his flashlight in the air. At the same time, like watching a split-screen motion picture, I saw Bill and Paul pointing their flashlights in the direction of Ike and me."

Rick watched as the three men gathered around his physical body.

"Bill started building a fire, and Ike was kneeling beside me with his flask, trying to get some whiskey past my lips and down my throat. Paul had removed my gloves and was rubbing my hands and fingers."

As Rick watched his physical self start to choke on

the whiskey, he felt his spirit presence in the garden with Jesus begin to waver.

"It was like every time that the physical me sputtered and choked, the spiritual me in the garden experienced a tug back toward Earth. I turned to say something to Jesus—you know, about how much I had always really loved him ever since I was a little kid—and all of a sudden I was being sucked back into the dark tunnel.

"The last thing that I remember seeing before I seemed to slam back into my body was the peaceful countenance of Jesus that emanated the most wonderful kind of love."

Rick suffered severe frostbite, and for a time the doctors felt that several digits from various toes and fingers would have to be amputated. Fortunately, his three friends had found him just a few degrees short of the crisis point and had carried him to their van, which, ironically, was parked near a clump of trees less than a hundred yards away. After Rick had become separated from the others, he had succumbed to the greenhorn hunter's curse and had walked in circles for hours before he became exhausted in the subzero weather.

"Not every one believes me when I tell them that I saw Jesus in that beautiful garden," Rick Kremer said. "Most people assume that I was hallucinating with the cold.

"But I am convinced that I had a genuine near-death experience and that my soul left my body and was greeted by Jesus in a garden in Heaven. I don't really care what others think. Lord willing, they will have their own opportunity to walk in the garden with Jesus when their souls are called home."

Encounters with Jesus or Other Holy Figures Are Often Reported by Near-Death Survivors

Encounters with Jesus, angels, and other holy figures are commonly reported during near-death experiences. Such researchers as Dr. Raymond Moody, Dr. Elisabeth Kubler-Ross, Dr. Kenneth Ring, and Dr. Phyllis Atwater have concurred that there is an astonishing similarity in the reports of those men and women who have "died" before being revived and returned to life through medical treatment. Among aspects of commonality in the experiences are such elements as the following:

- The near-death survivors report the sensation of moving rapidly through a long, dark tunnel before "popping" outside of their physical bodies. If they are in hospital rooms or other enclosures, they often float near the ceiling and watch medical teams attempting to revive their physical bodies.
- Many of these survivors state that they saw their life literally "flashing" before their eyes.
- They very often report having been welcomed to the other world by previously deceased friends or relatives.
- Whether or not they were of a religious background prior to the experience, they often report an encounter with a brilliant, intense white light that eventually assumes the form of an angel, a guide, a teacher, or a holy figure such as Mother Mary, Father Abraham, Jesus, or a Christlike being.

While it may be argued that the Light assumes whatever identity would be most comforting and reassuring to the near-death experiencer, those men and women who have survived such an adventure into the great mystery of death and who have been embraced or counseled by the image of Jesus remain firmly convinced that their experience was genuine and deeply meaningful.

In his earlier work on near-death experiences, *One with the Light,* Brad recounts the stories of a number of survivors who told of meeting Jesus on the Other Side. Here, greatly condensed, are just a few of those dramatic encounters:

During the Pain of Childbirth, She Felt the Comforting Hand of Jesus

In a lengthy letter dated June 20, 1976, Carli Van Buren told of the painful delivery that she underwent that brought her to the reassuring presence of Jesus.

> The light began to coalesce into a humanoid-type figure. I could begin to distinguish a face—eyes, mouth, nose . . . the image became that of Jesus—or at least my concept of how Jesus looks . . .
>
> His eyes were warm and kind, and I felt an overwhelming peace permeate every aspect of my being. His voice was soft and gentle.
>
> "It is not yet your time to come home, Carli," he told me. "Return to your body and to your baby. Remember that Divine Love is the one great power that moves the universe. Without it, there could not exist the wonderful harmony that exists in the celestial world of the spirit. Feel my Divine Love

flowing from me to your heart, mind, and soul. From this day forward, manifest the harmony of Divine Love in your thought, word, and deed and do all that you can to bring about happiness in the hearts of all those with whom you share your life."

Carli saw the image of Jesus raise his hand in the universal sign of peace and farewell. Just before his form disappeared, she heard him say, "Return now, my child. Return to your Earth body . . .

It Started as a Quick Spin Around the Block, But It Ended with a Visit to Heaven

On September 8, 1988, ten-year-old Randy Gehling of Arlington Heights, Illinois, was struck by a neighbor's automobile as he was trying out his new birthday bicycle. Later, after a three-hour surgery and many hours spent in the recovery room, Randy regained consciousness and told his parents of a visit to Heaven where he met his guardian angel, his maternal grandfather, and Jesus.

"I knew right away that it was Jesus . . . I knew by his eyes.

Randy couldn't quite remember all of the things that Jesus said, but he is certain of some of the words.

"Jesus said that I would never quite be the same as I was before I visited Heaven. He said that some of the power of the light would remain within me.

And he told me to let the love that I would feel in my heart express itself to all people.

"He said that I should never worry if people doubted my story or could not understand what I was telling them. 'One day,' Jesus said, 'everyone will come to see for themselves what you have seen.' "

A Near-Death Experience After a Vicious Assault Brings the Victim to the Arms of Jesus

The intruder was every woman's worst nightmare when he suddenly appeared from the darkness in the corner of Carol's bedroom. After the brutal rape and attempted murder, Carol was unconscious for three days.

Later, Carol said that her soul left her body immediately after her attacker struck her with a heavy, blunt object. Then it seemed as though she were traveling through the cosmos, faster than the speed of light, until she found herself in another dimension of time and space. It was here that she found herself sitting beneath an olive tree with Jesus.

> I say it was Jesus, because the being was so filled with light that it hurt even my spirit eyes to look directly at him . . .
>
> He told me that my spirit had been about to receive an illumination experience, that my physical and spiritual vibrations had been about to be raised. Often when this is about to occur, a negative being will be attracted to the positive vibra-

> tions. The man who attacked me had been possessed by such a negative being.

When Carol wondered why her angels hadn't intervened and protected her, Jesus answered that Satan was the Lord of Earth and exerted much power in the lower kingdoms. "Angels cannot interfere with the lessons that you choose to learn on Earth."

Carol could not avoid asking Jesus if she were dead since she was conversing with him in what she assumed was Heaven.

> "No, my child, you are not dead. Soon your angels will return you to your physical body, and you will be able to resume your destiny . . .
>
> ". . . You will be an apostle of Divine Love and you will teach many others by your example.
>
> "Divine Love is the one great power that moves the universe. Divine Love is the force that makes men and women think and do those things that create peace and goodwill.
>
> "On Earth . . . very few humans possess the full power of Divine Love—yet the influence of those few is felt all over the planet . . . It is only Divine Love that can alter the material and the animal in humans and awaken within them their godlike potential. It is only Divine Love that can transform the human into the angelic . . ."

CHAPTER THIRTY

✠

"Who Do You Say that I Am?"

When Jesus came into the country of Caesarea Philippi, he asked his disciples, saying, What do men say concerning me, that I am merely a son of man?

They said, There are some who say John the Baptist, others Elijah, and still others Jeremiah, or one of the prophets.

He said to them, Who do you say that I am?

Simon Peter answered, saying, You are the Christ, the Son of the living God.
Matthew 17:13–16

And they [the High Priests] said to him, If you are the Christ, tell us. He said to them, If I tell you,

you will not believe me . . . And they all said, Are you then the Son of God? Jesus said to them, You say that I am.

(Luke 22:67; 70)

Pilate asked him, saying, Are you the King of the Jews? He said to him, That is what you say.

(Luke 23:3) [All New Testament quotations from George M. Lamsa's translation of the Bible from the Aramaic]

Over the past two thousand years, the questions concerning the true identity of Jesus of Nazareth posed by the Sanhedrin, the supreme Jewish religious council, Pontius Pilate, the Roman governor of Judea, and Jesus himself may never have been completely resolved; but a nationwide poll conducted during the 1996 Christmas season affirmed that seventy-four percent of adult Americans "absolutely believe" that Jesus is not a figure from religious myth but was in fact a real person born two thousand years ago in the small town of Bethlehem.

The survey, sponsored by Scripps Howard News Service and the E. W. Scripps School of Journalism at Ohio University, also revealed such interesting attitudes toward Christmas and the story of Jesus' birth as the following:

- Sixty-two percent absolutely believe that Jesus was born to a virgin mother.
- Sixty-two percent absolutely believe that angels from heaven announced the birth to nearby shepherds.
- Sixty-four percent absolutely believe that three

wise men traveled from eastern lands to bring gifts to the child.

Unquestionably, the true identity of the man from Nazareth remains to be shaped and formed in the hearts and minds of the individual. The portraits of Jesus down through the centuries have been many, and the canvases of faith or doubt or honest inquiry continue to depict interpretations of his true identity that are nearly as varied as those who attempt to understand him.

Among the many characterizations of Jesus are the following:

- He was truly the only Son of God, the Messiah, the Christ, born of a virgin, his birth heralded by angels. The accounts of his miracles, his death on the cross, his resurrection, and his ascension to Heaven are to be taken as literal truths.
- He was a passionate, scholarly rabbi, well versed in the strict laws of Moses, who wished to reform the Judaism of his day. His parables and allegories were teaching devices designed to help the masses more easily comprehend difficult theological concepts. It is unlikely that he was crucified or put to death.
- He was a social reformer who became caught up in the more violent movement of rebellion against Roman occupation of Israel and contrary to his personal wishes became identified with the militant Zealots. He may have been executed as a potential troublemaker during a sweep of Jerusalem conducted by the harrassed Roman army.

- He was a teacher of enlightenment who became transformed spiritually by his intimate connection to the God Self and who sought to convince others to seek a heavenly rather than an earthly kingdom of peace. He was especially well received by the women who came to hear him teach a new gospel of liberation. The accounts of his miracles should be read as symbolic of deeper spiritual truths.
- He was a member of a spiritual community, such as that of the Essenes in Qumran who, after decades of meditation, solitude, fasting, and prayer, became "christed" when he received cosmic consciousness and became at-one with God. Proclaiming that the Kingdom of God existed within all people who would hear and recognize this great truth, he offered his own example and methods of spiritual accomplishment as "the way" by which all sincere seekers might "do likewise" and replicate—and even increase—the miracles that he performed.

While the strict, orthodox Christian may be dismayed that there could be even one alternative view to that of Jesus, only Son of God, it seems that the most hardened skeptic would have to concede that any single individual who could impact two thousand years of history has to have a power that far exceeds the ordinary.

French orientalist Ernest Renan declared that "all history is incomprehensible without Christ."

Theologian and reformer Martin Luther once wrote: "In his life, Jesus Christ is an example, showing us how to live; in his death, he is a sacrifice, giving satisfaction for our sins; in his resurrection, a conqueror; in his ascension, a king; in his intercession, a high priest."

To author Alice French, Jesus stands at the absolute center of humanity, the one completely harmonious man, "unfolding all which was in humanity, equally and fully on all sides, the only one in whom the real and the ideal met and were absolutely one." Jesus Christ is "the absolute and perfect truth, the highest that humanity can reach; at once its perfect image and supreme Lord."

American philosopher Ralph Waldo Emerson proclaimed, "An era in human history is the life of Jesus, and its immense influence for good leaves all the perversion and superstition that has accrued almost harmless."

Blaise Pascal, French mathematician and philosopher, was assured that Jesus Christ is a God whom "we can approach without pride—and before whom we may abase ourselves without despair."

And even a warrior, a man of action and conquest such as Napoleon Bonaparte took time to consider the enigma of Jesus' existence: "The nature of Christ's existence is mysterious, I admit; but this mystery meets the wants of man. Reject it and the world is an inexplicable riddle; believe it, and the history of our race is satisfactorily explained."

Christian Fundamentalism Versus Academic Theology

Over the past two hundred years, academic Christian theology has been understanding the life and teachings of Jesus as something far more symbolic and collective than the tenets of belief that Christian Fundamentalism proclaims as orthodoxy (that is, the

Bible as the inerrant word of God; the virgin birth of Jesus in Bethlehem; the validity of Jesus' miracles; his sacrificial death on the cross that atoned to God for the sins of humankind; his physical resurrection from the tomb).

In 1835, David Friedrich Strauss published his major work, *The Life of Jesus,* and, according to Bruce Chilton writing in the December 1996 issue of *Bible Review,* challenged Christian orthodoxy by stating that in the Gospels Jesus "embodies the synthesis between divinity and humanity" and the works of the Apostles "should be read as symbol, not as literal history."

Twenty-four years later, when Charles Darwin published *On the Origin of Species* in 1859, the concept of evolution led many academic theologians to consider the possibility that the true significance of certain aspects of the Scriptures could be reinterpreted in the light of modern knowledge.

In the first half of our own century, Chilton cites the work of such Christian "Modernists" as Alfred Loisy, a French priest who "doubted the Virgin Birth of Jesus, saw Jesus' miracles as symbols, did not believe God needed a payment in blood in order to love us and overtly denied resurrection in the same body. For him, the meaning of the Gospels resided in their capacity to transform our collective existence."

Baptist scholar Walter Rauschenbusch, who taught at the Rochester Theological Seminary in 1897, believed that Jesus taught a "social gospel" and therefore established Christianity "to change totally the nature of our social life on behalf of justice."

In the 1990s, those who favor a fundamentalist view of Jesus and his gospel have had to contend with the Bible scholars who meet annually for their

Jesus Seminar and proclaim such hotly received ideas as the assertion that the historical Jesus did not preach salvation from sin, probably never delivered the Sermon on the Mount, performed no miracles, and quite likely had no intention of declaring himself as the Messiah, the Christ, the only Son of God.

Time magazine (January 10, 1994) in commenting on the controversial book *Jesus: A Revolutionary Biography* by John Dominic Crossan, a Bible scholar at DePaul University, states that for him, Jesus' deification was akin to the worship of Augustus Caesar—a mixture of myth, propaganda, and social convention.

> Christ's pedigree—his virgin birth in Bethlehem . . . home of his reputed ancestor King David—is retrospective mythmaking by writers who had already decided on the transcendental importance of the adult Jesus.

Bruce Chilton concludes his article in *Bible Review* by asserting that "Christian theology in its origins rejected literalism as an approach to Scripture":

> St. Paul was emphatic that "the letter kills, while the Spirit gives life" (2 Corinthians 3:6). Classical Christianity strongly maintained that the fundamental basis of faith is not literal at all, but a link between our spirit and God's.

It is neither our purpose nor our desire in this present book to become embroiled in controversial discussions as to a preference for a literal or a symbolic interpretation of the miracles and mystery of Jesus as portrayed in the gospels of Matthew, Mark, Luke, and John. It is clear to us that the enigma of Jesus of

Nazareth may never be resolved to the satisfaction of both scholars and laypersons. To paraphrase the plaint of the character of Mary Magdalene in *Jesus Christ Superstar*, a good many men and women *still* don't know how to love Him.

Can We Receive Personal Messages and Appearances from Jesus?

When we asked a Protestant clergyman for his opinion regarding the appearance of Jesus and his continuing revelations to contemporary men and women, he did not respond warmly to our query.

"First of all," he began solemnly, "I believe that revelation has been given uniquely in the Bible and supremely in Jesus Christ—the only way to God, the one mediator between God and Man. I deny that there are continuing revelations from Jesus.

"Now, of course, I do not deny that there are continuing spiritual conversions and dramatic changes that are brought about through the proclamation of the one revelation of Jesus Christ through the word of God," he clarified, "and I am very excited whenever I see that change take place."

But what about those sincere men and women who feel that Jesus appeared to them, gave them strength and courage, perhaps even a personal message of inspiration? Isn't it at least possible that Jesus could accomplish such tasks if he chose to do so?

The clergyman shook his head. "There can be the continued illumination of individuals through the one unique and final revelation given us in the Bible and in Jesus Christ, but revelation has been completed and the Bible and the canon is closed. Any attempt to add revelations is to be rejected."

Then, after a moment of reflection, he added, "At the same time, I would be the first to admit that God continues to work and to speak in each generation and that He makes His word known today through the Holy Spirit. It is this same Holy Spirit that can enlighten and illumine people and bring them to conversion in Jesus."

The pastor went on to tell us how he had come to a personal faith in Jesus through an evangelical Christian youth organization.

"I accepted Jesus as more than a good man and a good teacher. He was the Christ, the Son of the Living God, who was born of the Virgin Mary. He died by the act of his own will, as well as the actions of sinful men, for the sins of the world, a substitutionary atonement on the cross. He was resurrected from the dead three days later, leaving the tomb empty. As a historical fact, he appeared to his disciples for forty days, then ascended in Heaven, where he reigns at the right hand of God.

"It was that message that brought me into the vital, personal relationship with Jesus Christ. And the thing that was most important to me in my own conversion experience was that message that Jesus loves me, that he gave himself for me, that he could come to my life personally and really change my life if I would allow him to do so."

We wondered if we hadn't hit a semantic snag in our conversation with the clergyman. If he believed that Jesus could come into his life "personally," how did that differ from those sincere individuals who told us that Jesus had appeared to them to heal them or to give them personal messages of hope?

"In those cases you describe," the pastor seemed

certain, "that is the Holy Spirit working through the Gospel power of Jesus Christ."

But if he believed in the Trinity—Father–Son–Holy Ghost as One—how could he be so certain which aspect of his Triune God was manifesting to men and women in need of spiritual succor?

Surely he had witnessed miracles during the course of his ministry, supernatural acts that defied mundane explanations and gave evidence of Divine intervention?

He was with us on this. "I have seen people given up for dead by their loved ones. I have witnessed people transformed and receive a new life.

"When I was doing youth work, I saw kids come off heroin, cold, just like that. I remember working with a young man some years back who had dropped acid over 500 times and who was also shooting heroin. He accepted Jesus as his personal savior and went on to get a 3.5 grade average in college. His parents, everyone he knew had given up on him. Jesus Christ changed his life."

It seemed that we had reached an impasse in our conversation. We were all celebrating acts of physical rejuvenation and spiritual rebirth through the power of Jesus' name or his presence or his timeless, transformative energy, but we could not agree on His ability to manifest outside of the doctrinal confines of a particular faith.

The Central Christian Experience Is an Encounter with the Risen Lord

In his book *Pagans and Christians,* Robin Lane Fox, a fellow of New College, Oxford, and a university lecturer in ancient history, emphasizes that epiphanies and visionary experiences constitute a constant part of Christian life, from the first vision of angels at the tomb on resurrection morning to the continuing appearances of Mother Mary and Jesus today. Already in Jesus' time, "epiphany and visionary experience accompanied his baptism and commission and recurred in the Transfiguration."

The Transfiguration that occurred to Jesus on a high mountain (probably Mt. Hermon) was accomplished to demonstrate his divine nature to his disciples. "[Jesus] was transfigured before them: and his face did shine as the sun, and his raiment was white as the light." (Matthew 17:2) The august figures of Moses and Elijah manifested to acknowledge their approval of Jesus and a voice from out of a bright cloud said, "This is my beloved Son, in whom I am well pleased; hear ye him." The entire marvel was witnessed by three disciples, Peter, James, and John.

The Transfiguration, Robin Lane Fox writes, was understood in terms of the epiphanies of Jewish Scripture and apocalyptic texts:

> This tradition helped to express, but itself did not create, the central Christian experience, an encounter with the risen Lord. In the pagan world, visions of a person soon after death were not uncommon . . . the ancients had their ghost stories . . . Christians, however, advanced the extreme claim that the object of their visions had risen physically from the dead. Visions of him abounded. Some ten years later, Paul was taught in Jerusalem that Christ had been "seen" by Peter, then by the Twelve, then by more than five hundred brethren at one time, then by James, then by all the Apostles.

Lane Fox says that while the early Christians had an ample tradition of epiphanies to draw on in their own Jewish scriptures, with the many stories of mortals meeting angels unaware, the "Christ epiphany" is marked by a lack of fear as the vision of Jesus intimately calls the individual's name and creates at once an aura of peace. Stephen, the first Christian martyr, sees Jesus standing at the right hand of God as he is about to be stoned to death and dies uttering a prayer of forgiveness for his murderers.

Thus, early Christianity was born from visionary experience:

> The experience caused conversion, a faith in only one God . . . At Jesus' baptism or Paul's blinding moment of vision, a heavenly voice and an appearance marked the start of a new career. The Apostles' own missionary impulse derived from their visions of the Lord after his death.

It seems to us, therefore, that contemporary encounters with Jesus among Christians and spiritually aware men and women of all paths should hardly be considered aspects of extraordinary behavior. On the contrary, such manifestations of our Lord Jesus should be expected and welcomed as a significant aspect of our spiritual heritage.

All Over the World, People Want to Be Part of the Christ Drama

What, then, should be our response to those sincere men and women who desire with all their heart, mind, and spirit to be somehow a part of the continuing drama of Jesus Christ?

Should they be open to the possibility of being able to receive revelations, comforting messages, manifestations of earthly healing, and promises of heavenly eternity from the loving image of Jesus?

Judging by the many letters that we receive and the countless personal testimonials that people share with us, we must express our opinion that throughout the planet, thousands of men and women earnestly wish to be a part of the continuing Christ Drama as it unfolds in our own contemporary era.

Although we do not wish to put words in his mouth or fashion images that might not be his, we think often of the answer of our friend Dr. Bruce Wrightsman, a professor of religion and physics at a Lutheran college, when we asked him whether or not Divine revelation was still possible and whether or not we should encourage such experiences.

"Oh, yes, we should definitely encourage the revelation experience in our lives," Dr. Wrightsman replied. "Without that, there is no knowledge of God. I think one who doesn't seek it is turning religion into a kind of moral code—and that's all he's got left.

"If there is no numinous experience, no encounter with the Divine, then all that's left is ten little rules for daily living—pretty sterile and pretty futile.

"I like to think of God as omnipresent in the human situation. The Spirit of God is always working, trying to open doors, confronting people, energizing them, enlivening them, seeking to create human beings out of Homo sapiens—human in the sense that Jesus was human with a humane, compassionate consciousness.

"The Jews were looking for a ruler, who would be just and fair. King David was their model. He was a scoundrel at times, but at least he was God's kind of man. Jesus came to show them that 'God's kind of man' is not necessarily a glorified military leader, but may be a man who can embody certain of those characteristics in a nonpolitical kingdom. *My kingdom is not of this world,* he kept telling his contemporaries: 'It's not the kind of kingdom you usually think about.'

"As far as Divine Revelation is concerned, from my Christian point of view, it's undeniable. I see too many evidences of it around, too many experiences of it in my own life. Not that there aren't other explanations available, but the other explanations are no more credible to me than the key word, revelation."

When Jesus asked his disciples what people were saying about his true identity, he asked a question that has been perplexing millions of human beings for two thousand years; even those sincere seekers who have no answer to the eternal query can sense the miracle and the wonder of this mysterious figure from ancient Nazareth. For those who accept the divinity of Jesus by faith alone, the question is easily resolved and they declare along with Peter that He is the Christ, the Son of the living God. For those who recognize a holy and devout master's achievement of the Christ Consciousness, Jesus is an eternally powerful energy source who transmits peace and love across the barriers of time and space.

But for all, those who believe or disbelieve, who worship or who deny, both the devout and the doubters, we suspect that there are few who, in their moments of strife and sorrow, would not gladly reach out and take the compassionate and comforting hand of an elder brother who promised always to be there and to walk beside us.

References and Resources

CHAPTER ONE: "LO, I AM WITH YOU ALWAYS"

Many of the personal accounts in this chapter and throughout the book are adapted from the personal reports of respondents to the *Steiger Questionnaire of Mystical, Paranormal, and UFO Experiences* that we have been distributing to readers of our books and to audience members of our lectures and seminars since 1967. If you are interested in participating in our ongoing research and obtaining such a questionnaire, send a stamped, self-addressed envelope to Timewalker Productions/PO Box 434/Forest City, Iowa 50436.

Sudden comprehensions or perceptions of a new reality, such as the manifestation of the spirit or presence of Jesus in the lives of our respondents, are sometimes called "epiphanies," so named after the Christian observation of the Feast of Epiphany, January 6, which celebrates the manifestation of Jesus' divine nature to the Gentiles as represented by the Three Magi.

For further study:

Bach, Marcus, *The Inner Ecstasy.* New York-Cleveland: World Publishing, 1969.

Halley, Henry H., *Halley's Bible Handbook.* Grand Rapids, MI: Zondervan, 1965.

Pelikan, Jaroslav, *Jesus Through the Centuries.* New York: Harper & Row, 1987.

Steiger, Brad, *Revelation: The Divine Fire.* Englewood Cliffs, NJ: Prentice-Hall, 1973.

White, John, *The Meeting of Science and Spirit.* New York: Paragon House, 1990.

CHAPTER TWO: DREAMS OF JESUS AND HIS ABIDING LOVE

Throughout humankind's history, dreams have often been cited as a means of communicating images and teachings of the Divine. The ancient Greeks and Romans believed that Asclepius, the god of medicine, would sometimes appear to sick people in their dreams and cure them or provide them with a healing regimen that they might follow. Devout Christians would be likely to maintain that all healing comes from God and attribute all cures to their faith in Jesus and their prayers for wellness. Consequently, dramatic cures that follow a dream of Jesus performing a healing are quite common among those who cherish his abiding love.

With the exception of the account provided by Dr. Barry Downing, the examples included in this chapter were adapted from respondents to *The Steiger Questionnaire.*

Dr. Barry Downing may be contacted in writing by addressing correspondence to Box 8655, Endwell, NY 13760.

For further reading:

Benson, Carmen, *Supernatural Dreams & Visions.* Plainfield, NJ: Logos, 1970.

Eliade, Mircea, *Myths, Dreams, and Mysteries.* New York, Evanston: Harper Torchbooks, 1967.

CHAPTER THREE: SAVED BY JESUS' AMAZING GRACE

We have heard many inspirational accounts from those who have followed the program established by Alcoholics Anonymous. Established in 1935, their general office is located at A.A. World Services, Inc., 475 Riverside Drive, 11th Floor, New York, NY 10115.

CHAPTER FOUR: JESUS BESTOWED THE GIFTS OF SPIRIT ON A SHY GUY

The Evangelist who shared his story for this chapter is a member of the Christian revivalistic movement known as Pentecostalism. "Reverend Bobby" believes in the baptism of the Holy Spirit, which may result in such spiritual gifts as glossolalia (speaking in tongues), prophecy, and healing.

For further reading:

Dyer, Luther B., *Tongues.* Jefferson City, MO: LeRoi, 1971.

Gaver, Jessyca Russell, *Pentecostalism.* New York: Award Books, 1971.

Gelpi, Donald L., *Pentecostalism.* New York, Paramus, NJ: Paulist Press, 1970.

Schlink, Basil, *Ruled by the Spirit.* Minneapolis: Bethany Fellowship, Dimensions Book, 1969.

CHAPTER FIVE: PRAYERS TO JESUS PROTECTED HER FROM A RAGING INFERNO

Prayer is a basic element of power within all forms of religious expression. According to a recent survey, Americans are great prayers. As reported in "USA Snapshots," *USA TODAY,* February 7, 1997: twenty-four percent pray more than once a day; thirty-one percent pray every day; ten percent pray several times a month; sixteen percent pray several times a week; nine percent pray several times a year. Only nine percent of those polled by Lutheran Brotherhood said that they never prayed.

CHAPTER SIX: ENCOUNTERING JESUS ON THE INTERSTATES

Many of these accounts of Jesus appearing on the highways are quite inspirational and, at the same time, suggest a strong belief that the Second Coming of Christ is near. The hope of the return of Jesus, also known as the Parousia, while believed to be imminent in the early days of the church, has, in mainstream Christianity, come to be largely replaced by an emphasis on the application of Jesus' words to develop a more spiritual lifestyle, rather than an earthly kingdom.

Those who hold to the belief that Jesus will physically come again and manifest the Millennium are known as "premillenarians." Once on the planet, according to the adherents of this belief construct, Jesus will raise from the dead the "elect," the chosen ones. These Christian eschatologists envision a period of one thousand years, as foretold in the book of Revelation, during which Satan will be imprisoned and peace and holy love will prevail on Earth. At the conclusion of Jesus' triumphal reign, all the dead of the Earth will be resurrected, the wicked sent to everlasting flames, and the just will live with Christ in a transformed heaven and redeemed Earth.

Postmillenarians differ in their perception of the event by their belief that Jesus will not return until after the thousand years of the Millennium have passed. While the general concept of a millennium is unpopular or rejected by most orthodox Christian church bodies, all Christian denominations believe in some form of a Second Coming of Jesus.

For further reading:

Cohn, Norman, *The Pursuit of the Millennium.* New York: Oxford University Press, 1970.

CHAPTER SEVEN: DOES THE SHROUD OF TURIN DEPICT THE TRUE IMAGE OF JESUS?

Frank Tribbe's fascinating article, "Apparitions of Jesus that Mimic the Shroud of Turin," appears in its entirety in the Winter/Spring 1993 issue of the *Quarterly Journal of Spiritual Frontiers Fellowship,* POB 7868/Philadelphia, PA 19101. His book is currently being revised for publication.

Address correspondence to: Frank Tribbe, 6415 E. Donnagail Drive, Penn Laird, VA 22846–9720.

CHAPTER EIGHT: A SPIRITUAL PSYCHOTHERAPIST SHARES HER MEETINGS WITH JESUS

Dr. Lorretta Ferrier may be contacted at The Center for Creative Change, 1716 Sombrero Drive, Las Vegas, NV 89109–2565.

CHAPTER NINE: JESUS GAVE HER ASSURANCE THAT HER BABY WOULD BE WELL

Healing and the casting out of evil spirits were paramount among the physical ministry of Jesus of Nazareth. It should come as no surprise that those who pray in the name of Jesus would expect healing blessings to follow.

For further reading:

Steiger, Sherry Hansen *The Power of Prayer to Heal and Transform Your Life.* New York: Signet-Visions, 1997.

CHAPTER TEN: THEY PRAYED TO JESUS UNTIL DAD RETURNED FROM THE BRINK OF DEATH

Contemporary medical research indicates more and more that the power of prayer to heal need no longer be regarded as just a matter of faith.

For further reading:

Dossey, Larry, *Healing Words: The Power of Prayer and the Practice of Medicine.* San Francisco: Harper San Francisco, 1993.

The monthly magazine *Guideposts* carries inspirational articles concerning the power of prayer and healing. Guideposts Associates, Inc., Seminary Hill Road, Carmel, NY 10512.

CHAPTER ELEVEN: AFTER A MIRACLE HEALING, SHE COULD HEAR THE VOICE OF JESUS

Beverly Hale Watson may be contacted at Sevenfold Peace Foundation, 2120 Pine Thicket Ct., Bedford, TX 76021.

CHAPTER TWELVE: CALLED TO BE A HEALING MINISTER WHEN HE WAS JUST FOURTEEN

Rev. Willard Fuller may be contacted at The Lively Stones Fellowship, POB 2007, Palatka, FL 32178.

CHAPTER THIRTEEN: HEALING IN THE NAME OF JESUS

A more extensive version of the interview with Olga Worrall appeared in *Other Dimensions,* a special issue magazine arranged by editorial consultant Brad Steiger and published in 1974 by Popular Library, a unit of CBS Publications, New York.

Lengthier explorations of the work of Dr. Cushing Smith and Agnes Sanford appeared in *Strange Powers of Healing* by Brad Steiger, Popular Library, 1968.

Brother Mandus' book, *This Wondrous Way of Life,* was published in London by L. N. Fowler & Co. Ltd., 1970.

For further reading:

Lawson, James Gilchrist, *Deeper Experiences of Famous Christians.* New York: Pyramid, 1970.

Villoldo, Alberto and Krippner, Stanley, *Healing States.* New York: Simon & Schuster, 1987.

CHAPTER FOURTEEN: ORAL ROBERTS PROJECTS CHRIST'S LOVE THROUGH THE LAYING ON OF HANDS

While the Old Testament has few accounts of faith healing, the New Testament contains the most well-known stories of miracle healings in the world. Jesus cured hundreds by the laying on of hands and the casting out of evil spirits. Since he tutored his disciples to carry on his work, a healing ministry was instituted by the early church and the power to heal was considered one of the gifts of spirit. As Olga Worrall complained in the previous chapter, certain denominations within the Christian church have not always remembered its mission to conduct healing services, but since the advent of the Charismatic Movement in the 1960s, increasingly large numbers of Protestant and Roman Catholic congregations have begun recognizing the power of prayer and the laying on of hands to heal their members.

Christian congregations such as the Pentecostals have always observed healing as one of the gifts of the Holy Spirit, and they take issue with their more fundamentalist fellow believers who maintain that God has ceased to reveal Himself to humankind. The healing ministry of Reverend Oral Roberts has been well documented and presented in numerous publications and media presentations. Contact: Oral Roberts University, 7777 S. Lewis Avenue, Tulsa, OK 74171.

For further reading:

Ferm, Vergilius, *Classics of Protestantism.* New York: Philosophical Library, 1959.

McPherson, Aimee Semple, *Fire from on High.* California: Heritage Communications, Foursquare Publications, 1969.

CHAPTER FIFTEEN: JESUS WAS HIS ROLE MODEL AS HEALER AND MYSTIC

Brad Steiger first became intrigued with the remarkable Brown Landone in the early 1960s and wrote of him in the book *Strange Powers of Healing* in 1968.

More than eighty American universities now offer formal training in the laying on of hands (therapeutic touch), primarily to nursing students. There are now an estimated thirty thousand practitioners of therapeutic touch in the United States, Canada, and over sixty-five other countries.

For further reading:

Freemantle, Anne. *The Protestant Mystics.* New York: New American Library, 1965.

Lewis, C.S., *Miracles.* New York: Macmillan, 1970.

CHAPTER SIXTEEN: A PORTRAIT OF JESUS THAT HEALS

Dr. Ingrid Sherman, the First Lady of Poetry Therapy, author of such books as *Gems from Above, Prayer Poems that Heal,* and *Radiations for Self-Help,* may be reached by correspondence at Peace of Mind Studio, 108 121st Avenue, Treasure Island, FL 33706.

When Dr. Sherman speaks of calling Jesus by his Hebrew name of Joshua, she is, of course, correct in calling our attention to the fact that the more familiar "Jesus" is a Greek rendering of the Hebrew name "Joshua," or, more completely, "Yehoshuah," (Jehovah is deliverance).

CHAPTER SEVENTEEN: THEIR PRAYERS TO JESUS CONQUERED A DEMON

The young women in this chapter are not alone in believing that an evil influence must be removed from the patient before true healing can occur. Charismatic Christian faith healers generally regard illness in terms of Jesus' ministry and practice healing techniques that summon the divine spirit to conquer the demons that prevent a complete cure.

While such concepts have been considered medieval by the majority of conventional allopathic and psychiatric healers, recently a number of psychiatrists have been boldly declaring that many people who appear to be mentally ill are actually possessed by demons or spirits of the dead.

For further reading:

Dickason, C. Fred, *Demon Possession and the Christian.* Westchester, IL: Crossways Books, 1987.

Hick, John, *Evil and the God of Love.* San Francisco: Harper & Row, 1977.

Harpur, Patrick, *Daimonic Reality.* London: Penguin Group, 1994.

Swedenborg, Emanuel, *Heaven and Its Wonders and Hell.* New York: Citadel, 1965.

Van Dusen, Wilson, *The Presence of Other Worlds.* New York: Harper & Row, 1974.

CHAPTER EIGHTEEN: WILL JESUS RETURN IN A SPACESHIP?

For further reading:

Nothdurft, Milton H., *Between Two Worlds.* Prescott Valley, AZ: Mountain Valley Press, 1985.
Steiger, Brad, *The Fellowship.* New York: Doubleday, 1988.
——, *The Gods of Aquarius.* New York: Harcourt Brace Jovanovich, 1976.
Steiger, Brad and Steiger, Sherry Hansen, *Starborn.* New York: Berkley, 1992.
Tuella, *Ashtar.* New Brunswick, NJ: Inner Light, 1994.

Dr. R. Leo Sprinkle may be contacted at 406½ South 21st Street, Laramie, WY 82070. Reverends Bob and Shirley Short conduct their ministry in Cornville, Arizona, and may be reached by writing to them at POB 332, Cornville, AZ 86325.

CHAPTER NINETEEN: ARMAGEDDON HAS ALREADY BEGUN AND TIME IS ACCELERATING

Armageddon is traditionally held to be the scene of the great final battle between the forces of good and evil. It surprises many to learn that far from a symbolic battleground, Armageddon is an actual place. The name Armageddon is the Latin adaptation of the Hebrew *har megiddo,* and refers to the mountain region of Megiddo in northern Israel.

For further reading:

Lilje, Hanns (tr. by Olive Wyon), *The Last Book of the Bible.* Philadelphia: Fortress Press, 1967.

McGinn, Bernard, *Anti-Christ.* New York: Harper Collins, 1994.

For information about the Love Corps, write to S.E.E. Publishing Co., 1556 Halford Avenue #288, Santa Clara, CA 95051.

CHAPTER TWENTY: CHRIST CONSCIOUSNESS AND THE NEW HUMAN

For further reading:

Fox, Matthew, *The Coming of the Cosmic Christ.* New York: Harper & Row, 1988.

Stace, Walter T. *The Teachings of the Mystics.* New York: New American Library, 1960.

Underhill, Evelyn. *Mysticism.* New York: Dutton, 1961.

Wennergren, Kristina. *Acting and Reacting in a Cosmic Way.* Tollered, Sweden: Regnbagsterapier, 1994.

John White may be reached at 60 Pound Ridge Road, Cheshire, CT 06410

CHAPTER TWENTY-ONE: AN ATTORNEY IN WASHINGTON, D.C., RECEIVES THE NEW GOSPELS OF JESUS

The new gospels from Jesus channeled through James Padgett were published in three volumes by the Church of the New Birth, POB 996, Benjamin Franklin Station, Washington, D.C. 20044. Brad Steiger wrote extensively of this work in *Revelation: The Divine Fire.*

CHAPTER TWENTY-TWO: THE CHRIST SPIRIT SPEAKS FROM A NEW HAMPSHIRE MOUNTAINTOP

Hapgood, Charles H., *Talks with Christ and His Teachers.* Turners Falls, MA: Threshold Books, 1981.

CHAPTER TWENTY-THREE: JESUS LED HER INTO THE LIGHT OF HIGHER AWARENESS

Brenda Montgomery may be reached by writing to her at 1860 12th Street, Los Osos, CA 93402.

CHAPTER TWENTY-FOUR: SHE JOINED JESUS ON A JOURNEY OF ASCENSION

In Christian belief, the Ascension refers to the departure of Jesus from the midst of his disciples forty days after his resurrection from the dead.

Liz Smith Anderson may be reached at Liberty, 2926 Forest Hills Cr., Rock Hill, SC 29732.

CHAPTER TWENTY-FIVE: A MESSAGE FROM JESUS REGARDING THE NEW ENERGIES MANIFESTING ON EARTH TODAY

Brenda Montgomery received this message from Jesus especially for this book.

CHAPTER TWENTY-SIX: AN EXERCISE FROM JESUS ON GROUNDING THE ASCENSION ENERGIES

The remarkable Brenda Montgomery shared this special exercise, which she received from the spirit of Jesus.

CHAPTER TWENTY-SEVEN: SUMMONING THE LIGHT WITHIN

Susanne B. Miller's book of daily exercises and meditations with the Master Jesus, *Summon the Light Within*, may be obtained from The New Atlantean Press, POB 9638, Santa Fe, NM 87504.

CHAPTER TWENTY-EIGHT: LORD, TEACH US HOW TO PRAY

For further reading:

Guideposts Associates, *The Unlimited Power of Prayer*. Carmel, New York: Guideposts, 1968.
Sherman, Harold, *How to Know What to Believe*. New York: Fawcett, 1976.

CHAPTER TWENTY-NINE: MEETING JESUS ON THE OTHER SIDE

Once again the accounts in this chapter were harvested from respondents' replies and comments to *The Steiger Questionnaire of Mystical, Paranormal, and UFO Experiences*.

For further reading:

Atwater, P.M.H., *Beyond the Light*. New York: Carol Publishing Group, 1994.
McDannell, Colleen & Lang, Bernhard, *Heaven, A History*. New York: Vintage, 1990.

Moody, Raymond A., *Life After Life.* Covington, GA: Mockingbird Books, 1975.

Ring, Kenneth, *Life at Death.* New York: Coward, McCann & Geoghegan, 1980.

Steiger, Brad, *One With the Light.* New York: Signet, 1994.

—— and Steiger, Sherry Hansen, *Children of the Light.* New York: Signet, 1995.

CHAPTER THIRTY: "WHO DO YOU SAY THAT I AM?"

Jesus' early followers titled him "Christ," which is derived from the Greek *christos,* a translation of the Hebrew *mashiakh,* the anointed one or Messiah. At first seen as the promised deliverer of Israel from Roman occupation and oppression, Jesus was later declared to be the redeemer of all humankind and the keeper of the keys of a heavenly kingdom not of this planet. In the opinion of many contemporary biblical critics, Jesus himself did not teach his disciples or anyone else that he was the Christ, the Messiah; rather, he offered God's salvation through the example of his words and his works. Such scholars as Rudolf Karl Bultmann stress that what should be important to Christians is Jesus' challenge to accept the gospel message and to obey its commands.

While the purpose of this present book is to present dramatic evidence of the power and timeless energy of Jesus and his ability to reach across all of history and touch the lives of modern men and women in life-altering ways, we list a number of books for further reading which present various answers to the eternally perplexing question, "Who do *you* say Jesus is?"

Crossan, John Dominic, *Jesus: A Revolutionary Biography.* San Francisco: Harper San Francisco, 1993.

Grant, Robert M. and Freedman, David Noel, *The Secret Sayings of Jesus.* New York: Barnes & Noble, 1993.

Hanh, Thich Nhat, *Living Buddha, Living Christ.* New York: Riverhead Books, 1995.

Potter, Charles Francis, *The Great Religious Leaders.* New York: Simon & Schuster, 1958.

Otto, Rudolf, *Mysticism East and West.* New York: Macmillan, 1970.

Mack, Burton L., *The Lost Gospel.* San Francisco: Harper San Francisco, 1993.

———, *Who Wrote the New Testament?* San Francisco: Harper Collins, 1995.

Robinson, James M., *The Nag Hammadi Library.* San Francisco: Harper & Row, 1981.

Smith, Morton, *The Secret Gospel.* Clearlake, CA: Dawn Horse Press, 1982.

———, *Jesus the Magician.* San Francisco: Harper & Row, 1978.

Suzuki, D.T., *Mysticism, Christian and Buddhist.* New York: Perennial, 1971.

Watts, Alan W., *Myth and Ritual in Christianity.* Boston: Beacon Paperbacks, 1968.